# TAINTED ELEGANCE

*Simply Beautiful*

COMPILED BY
## ASHLEY LOVE

Copyright © 2015 by Blooming Pen Press & Promotions

All rights reserved. No part of this book may be reproduced or transmitted in any form or by any means without written permission from the author.

ISBN-13: 978-0692386972
ISBN-10: 0692386971

Printed in USA.

To Contact Publisher:
Blooming Pen Press & Promotions
PO Box 68
Echo, LA 71330

# Contents

Tainted Elegance ............................................................................................1
    By: Sakira Baez

Trials, Perseverance and Faith ........................................................................4
    By: Anna Renault

The Price of Worth ......................................................................................13
    By: Ashley Humphrey

Excerpt from "Today's Top Story is a Four-Letter Word,
Messages from Spirit" ..................................................................................16
    By: Geri Hearne

A flower is blooming ...................................................................................18
    By: Huniie Parker

Beauty is NOT Just Beauty ..........................................................................20
    By: Phoenyx Tolbert

Positioned and Prepared ..............................................................................21
    By: Vernessa Blackwell

I Apologize to Myself ..................................................................................34
    By: Huniie Parker

The bricks crumpled ....................................................................................36
    By: Huniie Parker

Isadshi-Koseshi female warrior arises ..................................................39
    By: Huniie Parker

The P.E.A.R.L.S Within You...............................................................43
    By Jamie J. Brown

Alive..............................................................................................................51
    By: Granny Brown

My Healers!...............................................................................................53
    By Aliah Kinard

Reflections.................................................................................................55
    By: LaDonna Marie

Strength of a woman ...............................................................................57
    By: LaDonna Marie

Determination..........................................................................................61
    By: Linda Ponthier

No Longer Stolen .....................................................................................62
    By: Lyneise Rachelle

No Ordinary Love....................................................................................67
    By Marcella D. Moore (CellaD motivates)

Masterpiece ...............................................................................................76
    By: Desh Dixon

3 Excerpts ..................................................................................................81
    By: Rustie McDonald

P.R.O. (Pushing Resilience Over) .......................................................... 84
By: Serena Dorsey

Her .......................................................................................................... 90
By: Sorena Eaddy

I Am Beautiful ...................................................................................... 93
By: Vanessa J. Ross

Convict Lover ....................................................................................... 94
By: Terri Melissa Campbell

Tainted Elegance – My Story ............................................................... 99
By: Terri LaPoint

Love Is My Superpower ...................................................................... 102
By: Toy Parker

My Angel Watching Over Me ............................................................. 110
By: Vanessa J. Ross

A Letter to 14 Year Old Yvette ........................................................... 111
By: Yvette Jordan

How I Learned To Love My Body – "Imperfections" and All .......... 115
By: Nicole Eastman

The Girl in the Mirror ........................................................................ 121
By: Wilma Harris

You ....................................................................................................... 122
By: Ashley Love

ABC ..................................................................................................... 123
    *By: Takia Smith*

Beauty ................................................................................................ 132
    *By: Charlene Day*

You God Driven Destiny ................................................................. 135
    *By Cee Cee H. Caldwell-Miller. MA, CLC, ALS*

Undeniably Miserable ..................................................................... 138
    *By: Ashley Love*

# DEDICATION

I dedicate this book to all of the AMAZING women in my life:

My Lovely Mother, Nancy Brown

My Beautiful Aunt, Linda Ponthier

My Elegant Grandmother, Phyllis York
(My Angel watching over me)

My Princess, Victoria

My Ms. Independent, Amiyah

My Artistic Beauty, Phoenyx

& To all of the Co-Authors who share their poems and stories on the following pages. You are all beautiful and unique. I love each of you and thank you so much for sharing your stories, messages, gifts, and talents with the world.

Ohhhh, and I can't forget YOU (The Reader)!
You are divine and stunning! Never stop dreaming and believing that the best is yet to come!

# A Note from Ashley

Dear Beautiful Reader -

I am so excited that you have picked up this book. I got the idea to compile it as I was speaking with women who had been bullied and abused during the compilation of my first book, Fearless Poets Against Bullying. I found that as women grew their confidence and self-love that they no longer let things like negativity, bullying, abuse, etc. hold them captive in their own life.

I wanted women to have the opportunity to express their feelings around beauty and share their journey towards being confident in who they are. The women whose stories and poetry fill these pages spoke up with transparency in hopes to help change women's lives.

Enjoy the book and if something resonates with you, please post on social media using the hashtag #TaintedElegance.

You are Beautiful!

*Ashley Love*

# Tainted Elegance
## By: Sakira Baez

Tainted elegance,
Superior intelligence,
Women who are dutiful
Are more than positively beautiful.
Captivating beyond anyone realizes,
But true beauty comes in all shapes and sizes,
It's time for us to confess,
That our thinking may be a mess
When it comes to our shapes
Most of us wear superhero capes.
So many shoes to fill,
Doctors think the answer is in a pill
Or behind a needle or incision.
So many distractions squelch the vision.
Made in Gods image taken from mans rib,
We all start out as babies in some type of crib.
Somewhere in our lives, we make a decision
To embrace what we are or make our own rendition.
We talk about being empowered and embracing ourselves.
Yet, we allow jealousy and envy take over
To rule our lives and decide what is right.
Lose who we are
To a thief in the night
We need to embrace each other, lift one another up!
Realize that she is me and I am she!
Grace is ours in an overflowing cup!

That true beauty from within and it grows,
Radiates light.
Enraptures and encourages
Each other to do what is right!
Our circumstances do not define us.
What we like, or who we trust.
Your excuses will never help you,
Past, present, future,
All that you do!
You are more powerful then you realize, and
It has nothing to do with your waist size.
This is the legacy we choose to pass on.
The reflection of our daughters is found in the mirror of self, united in heart
To unconditionally love and accept each beautiful "flaw" that sets us apart.
Rejecting a vision of right and wrong,
A voice rises up in unison an angelic song
Of one accord
Declaring freedom to love each other, love ourselves,
And remember that she is me
And I am she!
Nothing we can buy and nothing sells
Priceless and powerful as the picture of "we"!!!

# About Sakira Baez

Sakira Baez, independent distributor for It Works Global, mother to four children, homeschooling mom, published by Who's Who Among International Poets, reformed and restored former criminal, faith based minister of Christ uses her experience to bring passion to her writing. She has been keeping diaries of her writing, poetry, and songs since she was eleven using the depth of her emotions to move people's souls to embrace each other and remember our foundation in Christ. It is through this eloquence of words, she captures people's hearts and restores their spirit and confidence in the mission to love others as yourself and work towards the common good of humanity to be single minded, one purpose, one heart, one mission.

# Trials, Perseverance and Faith
## By: Anna Renault

Once upon a time I was a young girl with big dreams. That young girl started writing little poems with visions of writing longer poems and even books full of poems. This lifelong dream continued for years before life seemed to get in the way.

Reality resulted in an early marriage that created a new dream. With love in my heart and a twinkle in my eye, I married the neighborhood bad-boy. He was good looking (like Elvis) and adventurous (like Peter Pan) that produced sugar plums and knights-in-shining-armor that danced in my dreams. I envisioned happiness and togetherness that I had witnessed in other marriages in my neighborhood. I could see us sitting at the breakfast table eating pancakes or eggs that I made.

Ah, the visions were awesome… Taking long walks in the woods, like we did while we dated… Cuddling on the sofa and watching a movie that would bring tears to my eyes… and of course, making love to produce a passel of children who would grow up looking like us, being happy like us and being the joy of our older years.

After nine months of marriage, I got pregnant and ten months later our daughter was born. It was New Year's Eve as opposed to my Thanksgiving Day due date. We were facing a new year and a new journey in our lives. Sadly, all the plans for and my dreams of a happy family came to a screeching halt! While the man I loved said he wanted children, apparently he wanted them in name only – not in the real world of hunger pains, crying and making bottles of formulas; and most certainly not in the realm of dirty diapers along with all the other things an infant needs.

Now, I also have to admit that when my husband and I married, I knew he frequented local bars – especially on Friday or Saturday nights. It was fun to go out, meet folks, hear music, and dance. However, now with an infant needing care and attention, I could no longer go along for the socializing, dancing and fun of being out. There was never enough money to spend at the bar; and we certainly didn't have extra money for babysitters.

Yet, my husband didn't see the joy in staying home. Somehow he always found money to spend, even if it was meant to pay the electric bill. He certainly didn't have any priority in playing with an infant that was forever changing day by day. He didn't see the joy of a first smile, or first roll-over or any of the other exciting firsts that a newborn experiences – all the firsts that will never be first again.

He preferred drinking and carousing in the bars. He was also a Dr. Jekyll and Mr. Hyde when he came home. That first year as new parents was tough and the drinking didn't help. Unfortunately, during year two – drugs found their way into the mix of partying along with the consumption of alcohol. Sadly, the mixture of alcohol and drugs brought out the physical violence for which Mr. Hyde was famous. Domestic violence entered our home and became a way of life.

The experience of domestic violence was something I had never known. During my childhood, what happened inside one's home was not necessarily talked about outside the home. When women had bruises or even a black-eye, there were excuses… "I bumped into a door!" "I fell down." "I tripped over the kids' toys." Always plausible excuses were used to explain the hints of any hidden violence. Some were believable, but over time, rumors circulated and whispers were sometimes heard about a drunken husband beating his wife.

Unfortunately, the rumors were often not confirmed with a few exceptions. The stories that were confirmed were often twisted to make the woman guilty of some infraction that warranted the violence. There were stories that the woman had not kept the house clean enough; or, that she didn't have dinner on the table as expected; or, the wife had the nerve to speak back to her husband. It seemed back then that these were acceptable reasons for a husband to punch his wife in the face – once or multiple times, doing damage to eyes, nose, lips and more.

As the attitude of the day was that the woman was always to blame for the violence, I began to examine my own behavior. Was I wrong in some way? Had I broken some unwritten rule of 'wife-hood' that warranted a black-eye, a cracked jaw, or a smashed nose? What could I do differently to make my husband into the loving, gentle man I thought I married?

The violence was also accompanied by jealousy. He constantly accused me of looking at or talking to other men. I went to work, but otherwise I started staying home. I avoided neighbors, the milkman and the mailman. I wanted to eliminate all contact with men – or at least as much as was feasible. For a period of time my husband even escorted me to the grocery store and laundromat after he accused me of going to there to meet men.

Life became unbearable. I tried twice to leave. Once I had the help of police officers after a neighbor had called them. My neighbor thought my husband had thrown me down the stairs. In fact, he had pushed me and I actually fell down the steps – carrying our two-year old daughter on my stomach as I went down the flight of stairs on my back. Upon arrival of the police, they questioned my husband in the dining room while I went upstairs, packed a few things for me and the baby and left.

I finally had to admit to my parents some of the facts of the abuse and asked to live with them while I sorted out my marriage. There were no domestic violence laws on the books. In court, the testimony of the police officers regarding the "fight" was not enough for the judge to issue a "separation for divorce decree" and my husband's agreement to attend Alcoholics Anonymous meetings resulted in me moving back home.

For months my husband attended the AA meetings and life was somewhat normal. Then, a couple of his AA buddies offered to celebrate his one year sobriety badge by going out for a few drinks. Hell returned to our house!

After another eighteen months of domestic violence, I noticed the impact the violence had on my daughter. It was then that I decided a permanent break was needed. It was also a time when my husband was not working full time.

I finally realized that we were making ends meet on my salary alone. I had to admit, against all belief at that time, that I could make it on my own financially as a single parent; and that I could live safe and secure without a man in the house. However, I still needed to find a way to either leave our home or get him to move out.

It was through the grace of God that my path crossed with a local lawyer who knew my husband from before we were married. After briefly describing the violence, the lawyer told me to have my husband visit the law office. I passed along the message to my husband who visited the lawyer. On his way home, my husband stopped at the bar – got drunk – came home and beat me for lying to the lawyer about what happens in our house.

Needless to say, the black-eye, busted lip and broken nose confirmed everything that I had said. The lawyer called my office the next day for an report on my husband's response to their meeting. He was told I was off sick. He called my house. When I answered the phone he asked for all the details. It seemed he could surmise everything that had happened. He sent someone to my house to take pictures of my face. He again left instructions for my husband to meet at the law office.

I was extremely fortunate that this particular lawyer was well-known in our area. He was known for being tough, and having a strong influence in the courts. The lawyer had a very short but serious conversation with my husband giving specific instructions about going straight home, packing his clothes and leaving our house. The consequence of not following orders was jail time.

The fact that my husband did follow orders – returning home without a side trip to the bar, going straight upstairs, packing his belongings and leaving without a word – is something that still amazes me decades later. I was in shock, yet relieved. I was surprised and excited to receive legal papers from the lawyer outlining our marital separation, visitation guidelines and even child support requirements.

For one month, my husband came on Saturday mornings to visit his daughter and to give me the child support payments. After that, I didn't see him again. I notified the lawyer and admitted that not seeing my husband and not receiving those payments was fine. I wouldn't have to live in fear of him showing up drunk; or, having my daughter sit and wait for someone who didn't bother to show up.

My life greatly improved as a single parent. I found that I did make enough money to pay my bills. I also joined a single parent organization that made it possible for my daughter and I to participate in various activities. For the next several years, we went bowling, roller skating, picnicking, and even camping. With group rates to events and swapping rides with other parents, my budget worked out beautifully.

Over the years, I sometimes used part of my paid vacation days from work to get a temp-agency job. This allowed me to earn an extra paycheck which then in turn paid for a brief vacation we took using my other paid-vacation-days! It is great to remember our trips to the ocean or the mountains. One year, that extra check paid for my daughter to attend summer camp.

The struggles of single parenthood taught me to stand on my own two feet. My accomplishments at work, which included a couple of promotions over the years – along with participating as an officer in our local union chapter as well as the professional association – also rebuilt my confidence in my own leadership abilities and highlighted my strengths and talents.

Thinking I was ready for another relationship after nine years, I married again. And while the second marriage did not include physical violence, I experience a small dose of mental abuse – a denigrating of leadership abilities and my participation in various groups. I was made to feel guilty for not devoting 100 percent of my time to my husband. I started backing off from participation in the various groups and committees. However, my husband used my volunteer time as his excuse for having an affair. He being 42; and, the woman was 22!

After 10 years of marriage, we separated and divorced. I quickly realized that no matter what I had done during our marriage, it was not my fault that my husband had decided to break his marriage vows. I bounced back easily and resumed my professional and union participation.

I was back! I knew I had worth. I knew I could be the best of who I am. I am me. The person God made me to be!

Having worked for the same government agency for nearly 32 years, I decided to retire and to pursue some life-long dreams. One of those dreams was to write poetry. It was time to follow that dream. It was time to put my past struggles away and to blossom.

For five years, I hosted a business of one, writing poems upon demand by customers who wanted a unique gift for anniversaries, birthdays, graduations, retirements and weddings. I enjoyed interviewing the customers and learning about the person who would receive the finished poem. I wrote poems. Found the perfect paper on which to print it or a frame in which to hang it. It was my dream come true… my time to shine, an opportunity to share my poetry with others.

Throughout those 32 years of full time employment and the five years of writing poetry, I also experienced multiple medical problems. There were several bouts of cancer, the diagnosis of my Lupus, and some troubling issues with my life-long heart condition. Throughout those trials, I allowed my faith to carry me through to wellness, to lean on the Lord and His promises to always be there for me.

In 2009, a bout with breast cancer put an end to my poetry business. However, I had also expanded my writing experience the year before – writing the editorial column for my local weekly newspaper (which I still do). In December 2010, as I won my battle with breast cancer, a dear friend sat me down to convince me it was time to write a book – a book about my life's journey through some serious and/or near death experiences.

"Anna's Journey: How many lives does one person get?" was published. The flood gates opened. That book lead to an internet radio show and several more books. Writing that first book helped me take a very close look at my life. I examined my experiences through which I discovered my talents, my strengths as well as the fact that the Lord has been very good at closing doors when the needed to be closed and opening others when appropriate.

My trust in and love of God has sustained me through the rough days of domestic violence, illness and serious accidents. It has been my faith that has been the guiding light and source of my strength to persevere through the many trials and tribulations life put on my path, tempering my resilience into steel! *Thank you, Lord!*

# About Anna Renault

Anna Renault is a daughter, sister, mother and grandmother. She likes to read and write. She writes for the local newspaper, The Avenue News - both in print and online (www.avenuenews.com). In 2008, Anna began writing a weekly editorial. Then, somefreelance writing and in 2012, a second weekly column was added, "On Health."

Anna also writes about cancer, the environment and the Bay Area Shuckers for Examiner.com; and for Readers Rock, an online magazine.

After working for 31+ years for the Maryland State Dept of Education, Div. of Rehabilitation, Anna retired to pursue her dream of writing poetry. For five years, she did that providing customers with personalized poems for special occasionsplus Valentine's Day, Mother's Day and various holidays.

Over the past 37 years, Anna has prayed to the Lord many times to carry her through serious illnesses and deadly events where she was present.

The Lord has answered her prayers and she is proud to stand-up for her belief and reliance on God's Will that she is still on this earth.

Since 2011, Anna's writing increased, accompanied by her blog-talk-radio show, Anna's Journey. She's published a total of twelve (12) books, each with a message. Severalwere written specifically as fundraising tools for her Catholic school alma mater, a local environmental groups and other interests such as cancer groups – the Cancer Support Foundation, the American Cancer Society, Relay for Life and the American Cancer Society Cancer Action Network. Please check her website: www.annarenault.com for more details.

# The Price of Worth
## By: Ashley Humphrey

How do we figure out the mathematics?
Adding based on the validation we get by men, striving to be called a dime or a ten,
When did we give men the authority to price our worth down to the cents?
When did we begin to thirst over attention not even worth buying?
We are trying to reach confidence from the pockets of men who are already broke.
Broken men who tell you what your worth will always be worthless because they don't have enough sense to see your worth more than cent,
Since I didn't know my worth, a dime seemed sufficient
His vision of me prisoned my ability to recognize my value so I accepted what I was commissioned,
I listened to a beholder who couldn't capture my beauty, he couldn't look pass my booty,
But truly I didn't care I just wanted someone to approve me
The approach didn't matter because my image of me was shattered I was battered and bruised from society's picture of perfection that I accepted anyone who would choose me,
Although I would know he wasn't right for me, he rightfully spoke the things I vitally needed to hear,
The sound of what I wanted to hear blinded me from what I needed to see,
Somewhere in between the blinks though, my intuition gave me a glimpse of the truth,
The proof was there but my confidence couldn't bear to take more abuse,

I continued to look the other way until I couldn't sway what I knew was coming,
I was running away but I had to face the fact that I wasn't worth more than a dime to him,
I finally woke up and could see that I was looking for my value in negative places,
Now I'm positive that no man can fill my empty space,
Beauty was always there but I wasn't looking at the true beholder,
God showed me who he was and I finally recognized who I was,
My worth is priceless.

# About Ashley Humphrey

Ashley Humphrey is a spoken word artist, poet, and painter from Memphis, Tennessee. Her artistic inspiration derives deep from the heart of art and music, Memphis. Humphrey currently resides in Waco, where she performs her poetry at different venues with other poets. She writes to encourage and inspire individuals to stay positive and overcome difficult life situations. With the influence of God's word, she strives to connect others through moving, relatable, and passion-filled poetry.

# Excerpt from "Today's Top Story is a Four-Letter Word, Messages from Spirit"

*By: Geri Hearne*

Learn to live within yourself, your family, your city, and your country; then, you can live better in your world.

Believe Me when I tell you it starts with yourself. Learn to live within yourself. That means loving yourself. How does one do that? By acknowledging hurts as they come up. By asking questions and more questions until you get an answer you can wrap your mind around. By doing that which you enjoy in spite of what others think about it. (Of course, I do not mean hurting another, unless that other wants to experience hurt.) You heal yourself by respecting your thoughts and cleaning up your vibration.

Do you know all is vibration? When you look at yourself and clean up how you are vibrating, you offer that same vibration out into the world. And then, that which you offer can only come back to you. So, look at this: You heal yourself and then you heal the world automatically. It starts with you. Don't go trying to fix the world, instead fix yourself. Yes, the man in the mirror.

Published by Balboa Press with Joy Media, LLC

# About Geri Hearne

Geri Hearne Chicago, Illinois gerihearne@sbcglobal.net 312-543-4079 www.heavencantwait.org www.joymediaonline.com

Geri Hearne is a veteran TV News writer, producer and reporter. She has worked in TV News rooms for 32 years, writing on the news of the day including politics, murders and war. Several years ago, Geri made a shift. Instead of reporting and writing on the world in news stories, she decided to share uplifting stories and is currently growing her own media company, Joy Media, for inspirational stories. Geri won awards for writing and producing both breaking news shows and reporting feature stories. She won several awards for reporting on the threats of dioxin to the Times Beach, Missouri community in the 1980's. She has several dozen Emmy Award nominations. Geri's latest book is about living a better life by loving more. "Today's Top Story is a Four-Letter Word" is about love. Her message is "Always bring forth love."

Geri is also a publisher. As creator of Joy Media, Geri has published several books, cd and dvd for other authors. Her own writing work includes: Paperback: Texas Trivia Quiz Book, Warner Books I am Beautiful Journal, Joy Media [coauthor] The Joy Journal, Joy Media ebooks: Here is Heaven The Wisdom Journal Working on: Cream Cheese for Your Roll and Other Stories From the Homefront

# A FLOWER IS BLOOMING
By: Huniie Parker

There was this flower
that was lying flat
on the ground it seemed to
be smashed
the leaves were broken
stem was damaged
it was dried up
from lack of water
and nutrients
until one day
someone came along
dug the poor flower up
and transplanted it
into a lovely
garden
where the owner had an awesome love
for the flowers in her garden
see this garden had other flowers
of all kinds,sizes and shapes
see all of these flowers
had been transplanted into the garden
at first the flower felt it didn't belong
but the other flowers started whispering to it
saying little encouraging words
little by little the flower started to heal
looking around at all the awesome flowers around it

daily it was feed and watered
and then one flower joined the garden
being transplanted there himself
he looked upon the flower
decided to drop some
miracle grow on it
at the same time
the others continued to
whisper and cheer it on
till one day
the little flower looked around
and noticed the others didn't seem so big any more .
it noticed it could breath better
it could feel the sun
to see that
because of all the love,support and encouragement
the other flowers showed
it had grown into one of the most
beautiful flowers in the garden
as the flower looked around
smiling at the one that dropped the miracle grow
it saw that it had finally found home
for now she was blooming
no longer dried out and broken
it had matured and grown
for now it had the highest honor a flower could have
it was BLOOMING..............

# Beauty is NOT Just Beauty
## By: Phoenyx Tolbert

I believe beauty is more than looks and a good figure. A person needs to be pretty on the inside. It is important to be kind and giving of yourself. Everyone is beautiful in their own way - No matter their skin color, shape or size. Beautiful is not something you have to learn to be. You are born beautiful. Love who you are and enjoy being you. There is no one else on the planet just like you.

Oftentimes, we like to talk, but we do not like to listen to others. Listening is very important when you are having a conversation with others. Smile. When you smile you help create positive in the world. When you frown, you are creating negative in the world.

Compliment people and it makes them happy, but do not forget to compliment yourself.

Like yourself so you can be happy and help make this world a happier place to live.

I may be young, but I know I can help people live a happy life by just giving of my time and being a role model to other girls my age. You are all beautiful and deserve success. Do not let anyone tell you that you any different!

Beauty is love.
Beauty is kindness.
Beauty is forgiveness.
Beauty is hope.
Beauty is happiness.
Beauty is me and Beauty is you.

# Positioned and Prepared
## By: Vernessa Blackwell

Lord I first want to thank God for this amazing opportunity from Ms Ashley Love.

My Continued Blessings to you. You are in Position and Prepared Glory to God for that.

Thank you for allowing me to be a part of this amazing Journey with such an amazing group of

Authors Tainted Elegance is a truly a blessing to me.

*I want to dedicate my chapter to my amazing sister who recently passed away.*

*Alicia Ruffin aka Lish.*

"You were so Beautiful to me. I miss your smile. I miss your infectious laugh, I miss the little things we use to do. Because of you I will not take another day for granted. I will live each day as if it is my last. I will live life to the fullest. You were amazing and I will always Love you!!!.

I am going through a transition of being a soldier for twenty years plus to a fulltime Entrepreneur which is not easy for me. As I step out in faith and boldly proclaim what my Daddy has for me. I pray my story encourages and motivates you to move forward with confidence with the vision God has placed inside of you

You are Beautiful Confident and Worthy. Why and How You are a child of the Most High God. He has made you a Queen.

**Move Forward with Faith Focus and Determination**

Loving oneself can bring about true healing and transformation. When I came across this poem I was so inspired, that I had to share this wonderful work of art with each and every one of you. With his powerful words filled with truth and intense emotion, Charlie Chaplin calls upon the reader to look upon themselves and ask, "Do I really love who I am and who I'm becoming?" I invite you all to breathe these words in and reflect on what it truly means to love yourself. Notice the world around you and how you relate to it.

**As I Began to Love Myself – A Poem on Self Love by Charlie Chaplin**

As I began to love myself I found that anguish and emotional sufferingare only warning signs that I was living against my own truth. Today, I know, this is "AUTHENTICITY".

As I began to love myself I understood how much it can offend somebody

As I try to force my desires on this person, even though I knew the timewas not right and the person was not ready for it, and even though thisperson was me.

Today I call it "RESPECT".

As I began to love myself I stopped craving for a different life,
and I could see that everything that surrounded
me was inviting me to grow.

Today I call it "MATURITY".

As I began to love myself I understood that at any circumstance,
I am in the right place at the right time, and everything happens
at the exactly right moment. So I could be calm.

Today I call it "SELF-CONFIDENCE".

As I began to love myself I quit steeling my own time,
and I stopped designing huge projects for the future.
Today, I only do what brings me joy and happiness,
things I love to do and that make my heart cheer, and I
do them in my own way and in my own rhythm.

Today I call it "SIMPLICITY".

As I began to love myself I freed myself of anything that is
no good for my health – food, people, things, situations,
and everything that drew me down and away from myself.
At first I called this attitude a healthy egoism.

Today I know it is "LOVE OF ONESELF".

As I began to love myself I quit trying to always be
right, and ever since I was wrong less of the time.

Today I discovered that is "MODESTY".

As I began to love myself I refused to go on living
in the past and worry about the future.
Now, I only live for the moment, where EVERYTHING
is happening.

Today I live each day, day by day, and I call it "FULFILLMENT".

As I began to love myself I recognized that my mind can disturb me
and it can make me sick. But As I connected it to my heart, my
mind became a valuable ally.

Today I call this
connection "WISDOM OF THE HEART".

We no longer need to fear arguments, confrontations or
any kind of problems with ourselves or others. Even stars
collide, and out of their crashing new worlds are born.

Today I know THAT IS "LIFE"

Proverbs 3:5-6 Trust in the LORD with all your heart and lean not on your own understanding; in all your ways submit to him, and he will make your paths straight.

Today, I would like us all to focus in on our talents, skills and abilities. I want each person reading this to focus in on what you like to do, what you can do best and if you could start a business what would be its mission.

In life we need to realize that we are not the issue, we are not the problem, and we were not created to hinder or harm others, but to love and help one another. When a creator creates something it answers an issue, solves a problem and bridges gaps to make things better.

We being created by God were also created for those very good reasons.

As we grow in life we tend to allow the circumstances and situations we faced as we matured from a child to an adult and sometimes decisions steer us in the wrong direction.

I would like to encourage each of you to believe that you can do all things through Christ; you can do all things that you set your mind, heart and soul too and you are an answer.

Often I ask folks what is your purpose? What do you like to do? What are your goals? What are your dreams? What are your needs? Wants? Desires?

A lot of times I walk away from folks with stuck faces or that need time to think about the questions I just asked. So I encourage you to write a plan so that you can position and prepare yourself at all times for what's next.

A lot of adults think it's too late to live out dreams or reach goals that they had when they were younger. A good percentage of our youth don't have enough positive role models so they end up on the wrong paths because as adults we should be responsible for the youth and lead them in positive manner.

We need to teach them that they have purpose and to tap into that purpose at an early age.

In reading the story of Esther and the story of Ruth, I read about two women 1 young and 1 middle age, both from rough paths. Esther was a young orphan who seemed to have all odds against her. Ruth was a foreign woman, widowed and broke. Both of their stories start out with a tough situation, neither knowing what their purpose was in life.

As they took steps of faith they soon discovered their purpose. Esther's purpose was to become Queen and be in position to save her people. Ruth purpose was to marry Boaz and get in position to be in the lineage that leads to Christ. Both of these women had to step out of their comfort zones and trust and believe in God.

Both of their stories paint a picture of how God can turn our situations around when we get aligned to our purpose.

I'm not sure what God has been saying to you, but I know that you were born on purpose, with purpose and for a purpose. So no matter if you are young or old, as long as you are still breathing you have a chance to make it better.

You have the chance to get your life on track. You control your next steps of your life by the decision you make on today! I encourage you to get positioned and prepared!

## Moving Forward: Checking My Baggage

*No man putteth a piece of new cloth unto an old garment, for that which is put in to fill it up taketh from the garment, and the rent is made worse. Neither do men put new wine into old bottles: else the bottles break, and the wine runneth out, and the bottles perish: but they put new wine into new bottles, and both are preserved.* **Matthew 9:16-17**

I wanted to prepare our minds, hearts and souls to realize where we were, where we are and where we need to be.

I would like everyone to begin reflecting on the people, places and things that have caused your life to become cluttered.

What areas in life do you need to rid yourself of some mess; baggage?

When I sat back at the end of 2014 and reflected on so many things that lead me up to the age of , I begin to see how in the past 5 years my life shifted in a new direction, but I couldn't get all that God had for me because I was steadily holding on to unnecessary baggage.

Striving to empower and help others at all times, but in my own life in dealing with certain people, in places and with things I still had stinking thinking and I still allowed my emotions to have dominion over my actions.

In my walk with God it may have appeared I had given my full life over to Him, but in reality I hadn't allowed Him to have every part of me. I had places I was comfortable in giving over to God, but then I had those places that I was uncomfortable in at all times, but held on to them, because I didn't want to allow God into those areas of my life.

I'm grateful that when I finally gave in and ask God to forgive me for my disobedience and meant it, there was a sudden breakthrough. The people in my life who had hurt me couldn't believe how much I had changed. They couldn't understand why I had no hate towards them and how I could be around them, when they really didn't want to be around me.

In focusing on the true matter at hand and that was living the best life that God had for me, I had to spiritually mature in all areas and I could no longer resist what God was doing in and through me, by limiting myself and keeping myself within a box in my thinking, doing and feeling. I couldn't allow unforgiveness or disobedience to hinder me from maturing in God.

So many of us are quick to want things to happen overnight, but I'm grateful that I allowed God to take my good and make it great, as He also took my bad and ugly and allowed me to learn how to live and walk humbly in humility.

Daily driving to the work I'm in praying mode, asking the Lord to speak to me and through me. As I was riding to work, a friend of mine had tagged me in her Facebook note.

While I was reading it, I felt as if God were speaking directly to me.

As I pray and look for a sign in a response from God and the title alone was on time.

In "It's Not Confusion, It's Transition"
Have you ever found yourself asking questions like, "Is this right thing to do?" or "Is this what you want me to do God?"

If you are anything like me, chances are you have. Over the past year as my relationship has grown with God, I have questioned my actions more and more. Most recently the decision on whether or not to continue on with my company Anointed Affairs Weddings and Events was one of the actions I questioned.

Those that know me personally know that it's been an up and down struggle with me for Anointed Affairs Late last year/early this year I was ready to walk away from Anointed Affairs. Unhappy with what I thought was a lack of success based on my own personal standards, I was ready to give up. After losing my last sibling. I have encountered a lot of emotional strain and and stress.

The devil had me thinking, "you don't know enough about business", you don't have the proper support system", "and enough people don't like you." Around this time is when I begin talking to God, asking for His guidance on the whole situation. I asked Him to either remove it or improve it, in short. I knew that my passion to continue on with Anointed Affairs was still there.

I was simply missing a key component, GOD!

## Checking the Baggage

When I focused in on Mr. Jolley's component that he was missing from his business, which was God, I began to identify all of the areas in my life that I had not given over to God. I began to develop a new plan to help prepare me as I transitioned even further along my journey in God. I thank God for using Mr. Jolley to speak to and to help encourage us all along our transition in 2014 and beyond by eliminating confusion. "I love his quote it only takes a minute to change your life."

In order to move forward from the confusion and transition there are places that you and I need to focus on that I call the baggage claim. Similar to the areas designated in the airports. When we travel by air, we are able to carry on luggage, but excessive luggage needs to be checked and received at the baggage claim once we get to our destination.

There are 3 key areas that I would like us to focus in on as we journey forward allowing our next move to God's best move in our lives that make up our baggage claim. The areas are thoughts, actions and emotions.

As we think of the baggage claim area and how it contains the items we could not carry on board the journey with us as we travel from our starting point to our destination; I want us to see it as your next move with God only will consist of what He allows in your carry on in your transition and the excessive luggage is your confusion; baggage.

Although the baggage may travel in another section of the plane, it is in excess of what is allowed to be carried on with us. Although we are able to redeem our baggage at the end of our flight, I want us to focus in on redeeming it only when necessary to be used by God in transparency.

We will be leaving our baggage in the baggage claim in 2015 and beyond. We will not get to our destinations and pick it up each time we journey forward. We will instead do as the Word says and cast our cares, in this case our baggage on Him. It will remain with God in our assigned baggage claim.

See there will be times when you and I tap back into that baggage because the baggage contains some of the good, bad and ugly experiences of yesterday in our lives, but has no permanent place in our tomorrow. We will need to revisit it at times in order to be transparent before others, but not to possess it.

As we journey along this year as necessary we will learn how to allow God to take us back down memory lane a time or two as we reposition ourselves for His will for our lives.

All in all He will be the owner of our baggage and we will just have access as needed to be transparent.

So I encourage you to purchase this book and encourage others to do so as well that you would like to grow in the things of God as we change our way of thinking, doing and feelings.

We will journey together and mature as Christians, Business owners and Leaders. Thank you "Jesus" for allowing me to be a part of Tainted Elegance.

As I strive to give myself a way to God I ask that each reader keep not only me in your prayers but all the readers around the world of the Word, all those who seek a deeper relationship with God, all those looking to serve God more, and all those in need. May we all be in the will of God for our lives; living out our God given purpose.

I challenge you today to position and prepare yourself for God's best move in this season! It's time we make go from good decisions to God decisions over our lives!

Be Encouraged,

Vernessa Blackwell

*For where two or three are gathered together in my name, there am I in the midst of them.* **Matthew 18:20**

*Father as it is written in 1 Peter 5:7 on today we cast our baggage on You; Father no longer will we play the game of tug of war with You on the things that confuse us and no longer has a place in our lives; Father whatever You see in us, on us or around us that is not of Your plan and we journey forward I ask that You remove it from us; Father send forth more people, places and things that are a part of the transition; as we transition from old to new; forgetting what is behind us, we press forward towards the goal in You! In Jesus name, Amen*

My Next Move Be God's Best Move.

As I step out in faith and boldly proclaim what my Daddy has for me. I pray my story encourages and motivates you to move forward with confidence with the vision God has placed inside of you. Ladies Get in Positioned and Prepared. The World needs what you have to offer.

# About Vernessa Blackwell

*I am an Author, Mother, Grandmother Soldier and CEO*

With over 15 years of event planning experience, Vernessa Blackwell, started Anointed Affairs Premier Eventsin 2007 because it is truly something she enjoys doing, and she was ready for a positive change in her life.

As the Deputy Commanding General's secretary for the Washington, D.C. National Guard, she had the opportunity to plan and coordinate corporate holiday parties, luncheons, briefings, retirement and promotion ceremonies and more. Additionally, Vernessa used her talents to negotiate contracts and work with vendors. Ultimately, she planned her best friend's wedding in just four months; and from there, she became known as the wedding and event planner among family and friends. Vernessa was inspired to enroll in the wedding and event professional course with the U.S. Career Institute where she ultimately graduated with honors.

Anointed Affairs specializes in Event planning, design and coordination, our services are tailored to each client's individual need. Anointed Affairs

Premier Events plan a host of events including networking socials, graduations and promotions and retirements. Vernessa and her staff's experience and expertise allow them to accommodate clients looking to plan upscale, large events, small, laidback beach events and everything in between. Their principle is that impeccable service should be affordable, and their goal is to give their clients the event of a lifetime, one that will leave guests raving for years to come.

With a passion to plan, organize and create events from initial concept to finished product, Anointed Affairs can coordinate and arrange all aspects of an event as well as provide day-of direction and implementation. You may know exactly what you want to take place and simply need a driving force to be sure it happens the way you envision. And if this is the case, you can trust Anointed Affairs to take full ownership of your vision while utilizing every resource available. On the other hand, if you have no clue how you want your event to flow or transpire, you may need them even more so. The staff's creative minds will come in handy as you prepare to entertain your guests for your special occasion. They also offer customized packages to suit your needs, budgets and desires.

Anointed Affairs' number one priority is you – the client! Their goal and desire is to build personal relationships with their clients in order to successfully implement the ideas and visions they want to make a reality. Allow Anointed Affairs to take the stress and anxiety off your shoulders. Contact them today to get started!

Anointed Affairs is one of DMV's premier wedding and special event companies.

Vernessa R. Blackwell of Anointed Affairs
Fabulous Designs for Every Budget
Phone 240 274-5549
Email: anointedaffairs@gmail.com

# I Apologize to Myself
## By: Huniie Parker

See self
I owe you an apology
I am the one that put everyone else before you
I am the one that hated you the most
See, I looked at how others treated you
Felt that you must have done something to deserve it
See I'm the one that got so caught up in pleasing that man
I forgot about you
When I got all caught up in everything the children needed
Allowing that man to hurt you when he busted your lip
Blacking your eye
No, it wasn't your fault he did
But what did I do to protect you
I apologize to you because
I didn't feel you were worthy of protecting
See everyone always talked about
How ugly and dumb you where
Even he said you deserved it
I didn't think you where worthy to be pampered
Or catered to as a Queen should be
I didn't even think you where a princess much less a Queen
And see self
I even allowed the wrong men to come into your life
Those men that just wanted to take from you
Steal in every way possible till they could suck you dry
Of your energy, your spirit, you love of life

You ideas, your dreams
Your very soul/spirit if possible
Even when the right man came along
I did everything I could to
Sabotage it
Then
Every time you got up brushed yourself off
Started back on your way
Climbing back up that mountain
I allowed it self
I apologize to you self
For every emotional, mental, physical and spiritual scar
I allowed
All I can do self is know
God had a greater plan
And even though those things happened
You are one awesome woman
I just apologize for my part
Self

# The Bricks Crumpled
## By: Huniie Parker

As I started to dig through the pile
Climbing that wall
My mind made up now
I felt one loose
This seemingly high wall
Had a weak spot

I shifted my armor a little
Made sure not a piece was loose
Gathered my weapons
After that wall I went
Breaking through was what was on mind

Remember to do as my Father had instructed
When in doubt remember his words
Him and my brother had given me
All I needed to go through

Chip after chip I saw fall
Little by little I went after that wall
Now don't get me wrong
I started to get tired
A part wanting to give up

Just as I thought those thoughts would consume me
I felt my help come

Not seeing anyone yet
I sat down for a break
Turned my back on the wall and everything else

Looking up to my Father
Trying not to loose faith
Tears starting to stream down my face
Reminding him of all he promised me
As from no where I heard

A sound
As if it was metal hitting brick
As I turned back to the wall
Someone touched my shoulder
Calling me by name

Never had I seen such a thing
Mouth dropping to my chest
The person was no less than 8 feet tall
Pointing me to the wall

As I dared to look
He bent low and whispered
I am his messenger and he said
"He would never leave you nor forsake you"
Now back to the wall

As I picked me and my tools up
Walked over to the wall
Got in the line between
Men, women and children
I started to feel something

A strength reaching up from deep inside
As with them I stood
Together we worked
Not a word was spoken
None was needed

For we were linked in spirit
I listened to the metal hitting the wall
Saw little pieces falling and flying
Then there was a crack that started at one end
As to my utter surprise

The bricks crumpled..............

# Isadshi-Koseshi Female Warrior Arises

By: Huniie Parker

I dragged my feet through the ashes
as I looked around me
head hung low
scalp shaved
all my glory was gone
as they snatched me
tied my hands and feet
and throwed me in the cage
time after time I escaped
fought war after war
molestation
rape
depression
attacked my body mind and soul
destroy her is the cry that arose around me
all the while sitting in my corner
head bowed
I called his name silently to myself
finding a strength they knew nothing of
I Isadshi-Koseshi
Female Warrior
hid withing
screaming
gathered my strength
studied my enemies

gathered my weapons
allowed them to think
I was defeated
let them pet my head
appeared harmless
as I gained in strength
while they took me through test after test
stripping me of all they thought they could
not understanding
like the Phoenix
I to will arise out of my ashes
as I step forth
strength arises
fills me
from the depth of my soul
he has poured out his anointing
has called me forth
with my sword
I arise
I stand
I am
Isadshi-Koseshi female warrior
Until it is my time
your attacks
only make me stronger
for I cannot be taken down
until HE says so

# About Huniie Parker

Huniie is MORE than a poet. Though she started out writing poetry as a teenager, as a way to escape the horror of being raped by her parents, and then foster parents, Huniie with God's help has turned not only it, but her many gifts and talents around to help 1,000's of others. Huniie is a spoken word artist, abstract painter, motivational speaker, publisher, manager of several artist, published author, organizer of others (Life coach, life strategist) . As well as proud mother and grandmother, Huniie has been interviewed international radio shows, interviewed and published in newsletters, newspapers, ezines, magazines, blogs etc around the world. She has performed on the same stage as Max Parthas, Tribal Raine, Georgia ME, Romeo De'Nati, Quietstorm of Spokenword, Blaq Ice, Urban VooDoo, Karama Sadaka, and many many more. Huniie has 3 cds and 3 published books under her belt with promises of many more to come. Huniie is the founder of HangOut 4 Artist a network of 1,000's of artist. Huniie is the owner of Writer's Nook Publishing, and Empowering Dynamic Families a community organization.

She has published 3 books, released 3 cds and has paintings hanging as far away as Germany. She has been involved in projects such as Stop the Violence, Stop Bullying, Against Domestic Violence, as well as an advocate for homeless, rape, child abuse, childhood sexual abuse, and domestic violence.

Huniie is definitely one you want to keep your eyes on with many more books and cds in the works.

# THE P.E.A.R.L.S WITHIN YOU
## By Jamie J. Brown

It was Eleanor Roosevelt, who said *"No one can make you feel inferior without your consent."* Imagine growing up in school where you felt different because you couldn't hear like everyone. Growing up in elementary, middle and high school was very challenging for me because I was set apart from everyone in my class. I was with my Deaf class for one hour and with my Hearing class for the remainder of the day with an interpreter who would follow me everywhere I went. I was picked on and bullied due to being "Deaf" and chubby. At that time, I felt like I had many factors that were wrong with me. I was black, Deaf, chubby and was a woman. But because I had a mom and dad that instilled in me some Christian values I was able to build confidence and self esteem from their love and support. The foundation of my confidence and self-esteem is rooted in my relationship with my God because I honor and have faith in Him. I live my life according to my faith in God. I have a family that accepts me for who I am. Deaf and all and a God that loves me more than anything.

As a Deaf/Hard-of-Hearing woman growing up I have been blessed to have a family that loves and accepts me for who I am. At first, I use to complain deep inside because I wasn't like everyone else. Why wasn't I blessed with two good ears? Why did I have to be this way? Why do I have to wear hearing aids to hear? Many questions of Why popped up. I use to say to my mom, why can't I be like you so I can hear? My mom patted her bed to motion for me to come sit next to her as she put her arm around me and said my dear, you were made the way God wanted you to be and just because you have a hearing loss doesn't stop me from loving you any less. I love you just the way you are. She showed me a scripture in the bible that stated that I was created in the image of God and that I was fearfully and wonderfully made. Those words still pierce my heart today as it did back then. From that point on, I knew I could do anything I put my mind too. Because she saw something in me that I didn't see in myself spoke volume to me. I am blessed to be the way I am. Blessed to be in both worlds. My left ear is my good hearing ear and my right ear which is my "Deaf ear". I truly believed that God created me this way to show people of all walks of Life that it's okay to be DIFFERENT.I am grateful He chose me to be a willing vessel to experience this journey; to be the bridge that merges the Deaf and Hearing world together. I see myself as an asset rather than a liability and a blessing rather than inferior.

Like many of you. I'm sure you were picked on for something. Either you were too tall, too short, big nose, blond, brunette, fat, skinny, black, white; Deaf, blind and the list goes on. But what matters the most is how you see yourself for who you are not what others think of you. At an early age I developed the self confidence that I wasn't going to allow people to walk over me due to my disability. It wasn't until high school that I learned the meaning of constructive criticism. I learned that I had to discern rather the criticism was constructive or not. To accept that what was told to me as a positive statement to help increase my character or reject it as a negative statement that would decrease my character. One thing you have to learn is people will be people and will have their opinions about everything; including YOU. You have to decide in your mind if you will apply it or reject it. The choice is always YOURS! You hold the key to your life.

I'm lead to encourage you and give you some words of inspiration to keep pressing forward in all you do. I love Pearls so much that I've created an acrostic for P.E.A.R.L.S. to continue to inspire you to greater heights to reach for your dreams. I'd like to share it with you.

P – Have **POSITIVE ATTITUDE**- You must have a positive attitude if you want to achieve anything in life. When you have a positive attitude it opens doors for new things to take place in your life. You begin to have a mindset of positive things happening. You see yourself achieving great things in life. Grasping the visual picture of you achieving that goal. Having a positive attitude is vital to your success, because when your attitude is set on positive things you can achieve more. You have so much negativity pulling you in so many directions that once you begin to think of rising higher you can go as far as the eye can see and beyond. I am convinced that attitude is the key to success or failure in any life's endeavors. Your attitude, your perspective, your outlook, how you feel about yourself, how you feel about other people; determines your priorities, your actions, and your values. Your attitude determines how you interact with other people and yourself. Be Positive, Be Inspired, Be YOU!

E- **ENCOURAGE** yourself and others- Learn to encourage yourself based on things that makes you happy; makes you smile. Those things that gives you joy! When you encourage other people you in turn encourage yourself. When you're in your valley, I encourage you to seek divine guidance from the spiritual realm. It is in those quiet moments when God is working on you; developing your character to be one of a kind. During that time is when your character is being scolded, molded, shaped, and crafted together to become stronger, wiser, and better. Respect the process of growth and embrace it. Always encourage yourself and others in the Lord.

A - **ACCEPT** yourself for who you are. You were created in the image of God. HE created you for a purpose. You are a Woman of Purpose. You were created to do great things. But here's the key. Do you believe it? Do you accept yourself for who you are? As you are? You have to accept yourself before you can do anything you want in life. You have to like yourself before anyone can like you. Who wants to be around someone that doesn't like themselves? Hmmm. Embrace all of you, exactly as you were created.

R - Be **RESILIENT** through your trials and triumphs. - No matter how hard it may seem. When life throws curve balls at you and throws lemons. You have to learn to take those lemons and make lemonade. You have to say I refuse to stay down for long. I will not be defeated by this situation. I will rise to the top. Learn how to bounce back when things don't go your way. You learn how strong you really are when God puts you through the test; the test of faith. Your test of faith says I trust you Lord to ordain my steps, guide me in your path righteousness and never depart from me as I'm embracing this challenge.

L- The **LEADER** within you. - You are a leader. Not a follower. You may not lead an organization or the nation or be a prominent leader or church choir director but you are a leader. You lead yourself. You lead your household. You lead your family. You may lead a group. You know when you are a leader when you have the power of positive influence on people. People are happy or they see themselves differently or have changed their ways based off something positive you instilled in them. That right there speaks volume. That's what a leader does. Empower people and encourage them to take that leap of faith to another level; to believe in themselves to greater heights.

S - You can be **SUCCESSFUL** at anything you put your mind to. When you accept yourself, have a positive attitude on life. You see yourself WINNING. You see yourself achieving great things you will be successful. Success means having the courage, the determination, and the will power to become the person you were meant to be. You are fearfully and wonderfully made in the image of God. See yourself as beautiful P.E.A.R.L.S. rising to the top. Above any obstacles that the enemy channels your way. Tap into the divine destiny that God has for you by getting in agreement with God for your life. Have faith in your own ability. You don't have to know everything or handle everything on your own, but if you tell yourself you are capable of doing something, you usually are! Look in the mirror, tell yourself you are beautiful, talented, brilliant, positive, and successful and you will be the best you can be!

In closing, I pray that you were inspired by something you read that will ignite a burning desire within your heart to confidently reach for your dreams, goals and desires. As you read the chapter along with quotes, affirmations and scriptures, declare by faith God will continue to build your confidence and self-esteem to a new level you have never seen before. Decree and Declare your P.E.A.R.L.S. are being developed daily and you are embracing the growth process. Decree and Declare you will not let anyone draw in negative defeat towards you that you will remain positive and focused. You are more than a conquer in Christ Jesus. Believe it and you shall receive it. God will see your dreams come to pass. Do you have faith as small as a mustard seed? That's all you need mixed in with a little hope and belief; God can do the rest. Be INSPIRED! Continued Blessings.

Quotes, Affirmations and Scriptures that continues to inspire my inner P.E.A.R.L.S.

## **QUOTES:**

"Someone's one opinion of you does NOT have to become your reality!"
– Les Brown

"The future belongs to those who believe in the beauty of their dreams."
- Eleanor Roosevelt

"All you need is deep within you waiting to unfold and reveal itself. All you have to do is be still and take time to seek for what is within, and you will surely find it" – Eileen Caddy

"Optimism is the faith that leads to achievement. Nothing can be done without hope and confidence." - Helen Keller

"Don't wait until everything is just right. It will never be perfect. There will always be challenges, obstacles and less than perfect conditions. So what. Get started now. With each step you take, you will grow stronger and stronger, more and more skilled, more and more self-confident and more and more successful." – Mark Victor Hansen

## **AFFIRMATIONS:**

*I live within my means without compromising my goals.

*I attract positive-minded people to me; I draw all things positive to myself.

*When I breath, I inhale confidence and exhale timidity

*I AM fulfilling my Divine Purpose in my life because I AM always connected to the Divine I AM.

## **SCRIPTURES**:

*1 John 4:4 New King James Version (NKJV) [4] You are of God, little children, and have overcome them, because He who is in you is greater than he who is in the world.

*Philippians 4:13 New King James Version (NKJV)
[13] I can do all things through Christ[a] **who strengthens me.**

*Romans 8:31 New King James Version (NKJV)
[31] What then shall we say to these things? If God *is* for us, who *can be* against us?

*Psalm 139:14 New King James Version (NKJV)

14 I will praise You, for I am fearfully *and* wonderfully made;[a]
Marvelous are Your works,
And *that* my soul knows very well.

*Genesis 1:27 New King James Version (NKJV)

27 So God created man in His *own* image; in the image of God He created him; male and female He created them.

# About Jamie J. Brown

Bio: Jamie J. Brown is a Floridian native who is Deaf/Hard of Hearing. She's bi-lingual in English and American Sign Language. She is an Entrepreneur, Motivational Speaker, Deaf Advocate, and Sign Language Interpreter by profession. This is her first book she co- authors' and she is no stranger to the art of writing. She can be reached at winwithjamie@gmail.com

Acknowledgement: I acknowledge this anthology chapter to God and my parents, James J. Brown (deceased) and Ida M. Brown. They are my reasons my P.E.A.R.L.S. shine and for that… I say THANK YOU!

# ALIVE
## By: Granny Brown

I stood in front of a long mirror and evaluated my body.

I started at my feet. My poor feet that burn like fire and are in constant pain. My feet and hands were affected by a combination of diabetes and chemotherapy. Doctors have suggested I have medicine to help with the pain. The possible side-effects are thoughts of suicide, allergies, kidney problems, strokes, etc. etc. etc.… I don't want to create more problems.

My legs are next in the mirror. The ugly bulging varicose veins dominate both legs. They ache and go numb. I use a cane to help me balance.

My eyes travel upwards to my stomach and the roadmap of scars. Down the middle is a long scar where surgeons removed the tumor in my colon that was full of cancer and ready to burst. The doctor removed the tumor and closed the colon off so it could heal.

On my left side, a hole was made to release my bowel movements. I had to put bags on the hole to catch my bowel movements. After six months of chemo, the doctor's scheduled a reversal operation. They opened up my colon and closed the whole in my stomach.

The sagging breasts were the next vision in the mirror. They sagged to my stomach and no bra could make these babies erect again.

Moving upwards to my neck is funny because I look like a relative to a turkey. My little granddaughter said, " Grandma, you have a gobbler like a turkey."

My face has suffered from sagging jaws from dentures that I have worn the last 20 years.

I can't see without my glasses and my eyelids sag badly.

The hair is like an old grey mare.

Am I depressed over my body? No, not at all because each sag, scar, wrinkle, and bulge means I have survived and I am ALIVE!

The mirror shows the battles that God has helped me get through to be here on earth.

My worn out body still has life in it. I am retired now, but I live in the country. I rake, pull weeds and plant flowers and vegetables.

My four year old granddaughter sums up what beauty is when she puts her little hand on my face and said, "Grandma, you are pretty." Beauty is in the eyes of the beholder. Take what God gave you and do the best you can.

Give of yourself to others and BE ALIVE!

# My Healers!
## By Aliah Kinard

Deep down inside,
There was sorrow and lies;
Frozen heart, teary eyes
confused in all areas of my life.
Felt I was always doing wrong
Never right.
Forced to my knees
on rose concrete so they bleed.
I feel like such a disgrace;
Head cemented to my hands
so you can't see my face.
Slowly time passed me by
Like a clock with no hands.
I saw life was worthwhile
So I look up to the Man.
The Man is my God,
My heart, My Soul.
'Cause I know he would never betray me
And never do me wrong.
He gave me the power to speak,
The power to rise off my hideous, scarred knees.
The power to rip my hands from my face
And feel Heaven's loving grace.
I opened my crystal brown eyes,
And finally realized, that it was you.
My family and God,

helping me through troubled times.
I appreciate that your love was always true to me
Now it's my turn to help the people who loved me.

~~~~~~

I may be Tainted, but I'm Simply Beautiful!

# REFLECTIONS
## By: LaDonna Marie

I press in
I hold my head up and
Fight to stay strong
God's word is my comfort
So I am alert of the worries
And anxieties of the world
That is around and tries to creep near
I sit and observe as the
Overwhelming feelings of pressure that
Try to overtake me
It is then when I begin to press in
I lean in
To the Lord
I feed my hungry heart and
Thirsty ears
With the seed of his word
To be filled
Learning all what he says
concerning his children
Then I bounce back
I am aware and see
The schemes and trickery
That is set for me to stumble and fall
Now I know I am more than a Conqueror
While pleading the blood
As I stay strong

See these distractions constantly try to get a reaction
Testing the old, that no longer lives here
So I press in
I am anxious for nothing
But in everything I pray
Petition with thanksgiving
And present the request to God
Reflections

# STRENGTH OF A WOMAN
## By: LaDonna Marie

I am she
I am she who have traveled
A long way to learn me
See the bible states Greater is he that is in me
And I fully agree
Yet many tears and many years
Have helped to define the character that is me
See I must admit
I have played the game hard
I have played the game fair
I looked for loop holes that just weren't there
Through the many challenges that I've faced
They have stretched my faith
They have strengthen my backbone
They have taught me Integrity
and most importantly
What is proper self care
So I am she
Who decided to that I had dig my self out the hole
The one I allowed others to placed my emotions in a dungeon
As they held the key
With viscous and fictitious words
That at one time where painful to my soul
So I began to learn the rules
That I had all power and authority
When it comes to me and the words I receive

So I am she who rises from the trenches
proudly waving my flag
Embrace the truth and all that I am
Representing the Strength of a woman
That show in my character
Signifying I better and not bitter
So words will no longer get the best of me!
For I am she
Representing the Strength of a woman

# About LaDonna Marie

LaDonna Marie is an Author, Writer, Poet, Co-host, and Motivational Speaker. She is originally from Mississippi and now lives in GA. She published her first poem in an anthology called: Whispers with The League of American Poets in 2007. In 2010 she self published her first book Expressions of the Mind, Body & Soul. She received a Certificate of Congratulation from Congressman Bennie Thompson 2nd district of MS. She was inducted Who's Who in Black Mississippi in 2012. LaDonna also received and Humanitarian award in 2012. In 2013 she released her 2nd book Until Tomorrow Comes, also was nominated for a Stiletto Woman in business award. In Nov. 2013 with her dedication to the youth she launched her first youth for Christ conference, called Planting Positive Seeds, to help motivate, encourage, and empower the youth.

LaDonna Marie has been featured in International Author Blog Interviews for South Africa, London, and Italy. LaDonna's first poem to music " I See You" was played on the Jazz soul radio in Australia. LaDonna Marie's Magazine Features includes SHINE, YOUnique, Precioustones, C. Hub, Image and Style, Blaq Rayn Poetry Publications, Honey Drip Radio Magazine and Sibyl Women Magazine. Until Tomorrow Comes made

Amazon Best Selling in Poetry and Personal Growth. Author LaDonna Marie is apart of the 2014 Anthology The Gospel According to Poetry, the Good Newz Project. Until Tomorrow Comes has been awarded Honorable Mention in the 2014 Paris Book Festival in Poetry Category and the 2014 DJ Gatsby Book Club Literary Award in Poetry. Her third book is entitled "Lessons: Shattered Pieces Being Restored" . She is a one of the finalists for The Diva Author international women's Award for the Divas of Colour 2015 in London.

# DETERMINATION
## By: Linda Ponthier

I am sixty-five years old and I am still going strong.

When I was young, life was taken for granted.

The body worked and I felt I had time to do all the things I wanted to do.

Life is short and before you know it your body starts wearing out.

My husband died and it was hard for me to continue on, but life goes on.

I had a heart attack and had to be patient and let my body heal.

Over the years, I have learned not to take life for granted.

In one minute, your health can change.

Be determined to live life to its fullest. Be kind to others, like yourself and never give up.

**Dream**
**Evolve**
**Think**
**Encourage**
**Remind Yourself (How Amazing You Are)**
**Mentor**
**Ignore (Negativity)**
**Never STOP Progressing**
**Eliminate Negative Words (From Your Vocabulary)**
**Die Empty (Share your gifts with the world)**

# NO LONGER STOLEN
## By: Lyneise Rachelle

You... you many are pioneers.
Paved ways down streets that aimed to bury your tortures, but...

I see you.

Successfully knowing nothing could succeed, because they failed self-education, so...

I learned you.

Punched out both eyes and placed them in deaf ears, now...

I hear you.

Turned your mother's milk into stone with witch-crafted fingerprints that only found the scales of her hands holding you near her bosom, because...

I need you.
Cry...
No one will ever feel.
So cry...
But...

I feel you.

Sweet lady skin vaselined up like a buttery biscuit.
They eat, they greed for more.
She mourns herself; yes...

I want you.

Here...
Take it.
Now.
All of whatever you so choose.
It is ALL yours and that is ALL good, and...

I...
Care...
For...
YOU.

Emotionless tonality.
Drowsy
Drunk
Switches switching, yes...

I understand you.

To my face...come
With it ALL...come
Speak your blunder and make the weak well.
We are switching, and now...

I will fight for you.

Sing the lullaby blues & reds, because...

I love you.

Handsome words...

I love you.

With no action...

We love you.

We...
do...
COME!

# *About Lyneise Rachelle*

As a shy little girl, Lyneise was, in her own way, always seeking other forms of effective communication. Picked on for being too smart and proper or misunderstood and called "weird" for her daring style and different mannerisms seemed to be the norm. Those adolescent years were the beginning stages of a well-groomed introvert.

With the encouragement of her family, she soon took a liking to fine arts such as painting and sculpting, classical music and musicals. Around age 12 a simple silly poem heard on television inspired her to become a writer; specifically a poet. Fascinated with stories written by her mother who is a ghost children's book writer, Lyneise began to free write in journals to create her own poetry and entered every contest she could find. Anxious and hopeful to win each one that anxiety quickly developed into doubt and fear of failure.

It wasn't too soon after that through her teenage years into adulthood, Lyneise experienced crucial ups and downs which paved the path for a more troubled life. "I've suffered through physical abuse, mental frustrations with self-blame for others faults and internal hatred for failing to successfully do better with my life. When it seemed like nothing would ever go as I had planned, I became suicidal and chronically depressed, but in my silence I learned that I didn't really want to die, nor remain unhappy. The moment I realized how my behaviors and thoughts were effecting my then 4 year old daughter, I decided to turn my life around. The journey was a tiresome one and there were many days I wanted to quit, but I knew I had a greater purpose."

Lyneise is a professional singer, songwriter and actress currently residing in the Miami, FL area. "Performing is a strong passion of mine. It is my release of everything that has ever ailed me. I am letting go each time I sing a note or get into character. Much like painting, for me, being a performer is like exposing my diary to whomever is willing to listen."

She had owned a real estate investment company for nearly 7 years and has an ongoing career of about 15 years in the field. Is a published author of poetry since early teen years (one particular poem "Ben Jermaine" gained her Editor's choice award for its suggestive historical content in the area of slavery) and will be completing her first poetry book in 2015. Her intrigue of the human mind from past personal relationships and observations in various capacities has sparked Lyneise to study Psychology and complete her self-help book. "I enjoy motivating people to seek out their own greatness. I'm not a perfect being, none of us are, but we can encourage one another when in proper frame of mind to do so. With a humble heart, a kind hand and at least one shoulder for the tears, I feel, we can certainly overcome any obstacle."

Now, as co-founder of a non-profit organization which focuses on the awareness, rehabilitation and prevention of crimes against children, Lyneise is afforded the ability to move forward with her passion for enhancing human life by advancing human thought.

# NO ORDINARY LOVE
### By Marcella D. Moore (CellaD motivates)

**NO ORDINARY LOVE**

There once was a love that seemed so far and untrue.
I never experienced it so when she knocked at my door,
I did not know what to do.
I opened the door and invited her in,
And as we spent time together, she felt like a friend.
She explained that she had been searching for me
For such a long time
But never gave up because the void was so strong,
And she knew that someday that I would come along.
She shared that her love was not ordinary
Because everything she touched
Became extraordinary.
She asked if I would be willing to take her in
And allow her to bring my searching to an end.
She assured me that she could fill the hole inside
That I met each and every night as I grabbed my pillow and cried.
At first I was shaken because this felt so strange, but then I
Remembered that I had just prayed for a change.
I opened my heart and let her in and began loving myself,
And she became my closest friend.
I vowed to this day that I would love myself first and honor the
Gift of me that God placed on this earth.
Today my life is forever changed
Because I embraced the power of no ordinary love, and
With this love my life is no longer the same.

Imagine, if in first grade, there was a class or subject called "Love Thyself." In a perfect world, this class would exist and teach the importance of self-love and caring for ourselves. Imagine that the core of the class would be to teach us to accept who we are and validate ourselves; the class would continue each year through the 12th grade. Part of the curriculum would include teaching the power of being true to ourselves. The class would have various speakers come in and talk about paying attention to intuition and the inner voice. The exams for the class would cause us to concentrate on ourselves and not to say yes when we want to say no. In another part of the class, we would be alone and appreciate who we are. The class would encourage us to search our gifts and nurture them each year. Finally, the class would teach us how to make and set goals for ourselves, and how to take action steps to ensure those goals are reached.

Unfortunately, this early learning ability does not exist, and most people don't learn to love and embrace themselves. People find themselves living life, searching for love in all of the wrong places. In addition to looking for love in all of the wrong places, many look to others for acceptance and validation.

When you spend your life feeling rejected and not loved, it causes you to make choices and decisions that don't necessarily serve your best interest. We stay in relationships that fail to make us better. We allow people to treat us badly, for the sake of having friends. We do things we really don't want to do and say yes when we really want to say no. This behavior is a result of not loving ourselves. The late poet, Maya Angelou, said, "If I am not good to myself, how can I expect anyone else to be good to me?" Basically, she's saying that we teach people how to treat us; therefore, if we don't love ourselves, how can we expect others to truly love us?

Are you seeing yourself as you read my words? How do you really feel about you? What do you mean to you? How important are you to you? You have to ask yourself these questions, and you have to be honest with your answers. We believe that treating others better than we treat ourselves is the right and loyal thing to do. But . . . is it? While this is not an attempt to impose my spiritual belief on you, it is an attempt to expose the love I have experienced through the One Who I believe created all things. I believe it is necessary for you to understand my foundation and basis that have allowed me to be clear about the love, which is necessary for me to live my life on purpose and love myself in a way that is not ordinary according to society. My spiritual foundation has played a significant part in my love journey, because I believe the awesome Creator has a love for me that goes far beyond the love any individual has for me.

There is a great commandment in the New Testament of the Bible that reads, "The second is this: 'Love your neighbor as yourself.'" St. Mark 12:31, New International Version. How can you love others when you don't love yourself?

The definition of love, according to Merriam-Webster dictionary, is "a feeling of strong or constant affection for a person; warm attachment, enthusiasm or devotion; an unselfish loyal and benevolent concern for the good of another." Do you feel this way about yourself? Most of us answer "NO!" This lack of love exists because we were never taught: "It is okay to love me." We seem to confuse selfishness with self-love; self-love is not being selfish.

If you want to change your life and want to live a life of abundance and success, the first choice has to be to love you and understand that doing so is not a bad thing. When you take care of you and love you, your mind is clearer, you make better choices, and you have a greater appreciation for life. If you have ever taken an airplane, you have experienced the safety presentation concerning the oxygen mask when the flight attendant says, "If you are traveling with a child or elderly person, put on your mask first and then serve them." Wow, how powerful is that! You can better assist others when you take care of and love you first.

Let me remind you of how powerful you really are. Your mother carried you, and when it was time for you to be born, you made your grand entrance onto this earth (regardless of your parents' situation or relationship), and you did so with purpose. The moment you exited your mother's womb, opened your mouth and cried, you made an announcement to the universe that you were here. For many of you, the cry still exists. You made the cry, but you never walked in the power of your announcement. You are here to love and be loved, to serve and be served, and to assist and be assisted. But more importantly, you are here to live a life of purpose. Discovering your purpose begins with loving the person who will carry out that purpose, and that person is you.

There is a love, which is not ordinary (normal or usual), you can begin giving yourself today. But the love that is awaiting you, for you, is special. It is unusual and it is different. It is not ordinary because in today's society, ordinary expects you to cater to and take care of everyone else before you even begin to look at yourself. The love you have been searching for is within you. It was placed in you the moment God dropped you in your mother's belly. The nose, the lips, the legs, the hands, the eyes, the hair, all of you, were included in that beautiful package, which was delivered to the world the day you were born. There is only one beautiful you; you have not been, nor can you be duplicated. Your voice, your smile, your laugh, and the special look you give to others at certain times, are all you. You are here on purpose, and regardless of what you have done in the past, purpose is still your name.

It is time for you to enter the "DO-OVER" mode, and in this mode you walk in courage by assessing your life and being real about what has and has not worked for you. You look at what you have left, not what you have lost, and you see the value in what is left. You take what is left and review the lessons of what is attached to it, and you begin living life, in and on the strength of those lessons. Many of those lessons say, "You are still here and because you are, you have the ability to do it over again in a powerful and effective way."

You are awesome, amazing, beautiful, creative, and God's masterpiece. When God sees you, He sees a reflection of Himself, which means all that He is, is in you. He sees the gifts, the talents, the heart, the ambition, the courage, and the strength that is in you. You have the right to walk in confidence. You have the right to embrace your journey, and you have the right to love yourself in a way that demands respect and love from others.

In a perfect world, you would have been raised to love and respect yourself and see yourself as the powerful change agent you are. However, because many of us were not privileged to experience a life that spoke confidence, courage, and strength, to us it appears we have lived life in an unproductive way. But may I tell you that today you have the ability to redesign, renovate, reset, and reverse your story. You are the author of your story, and God has given you the ability to write and create chapters of hope. Earlier, I mentioned the power of life lessons. These lessons, or what you may identify as mistakes, can be turned from stumbling blocks to stepping stones, which lead to your amazing "yellow brick road."

Now you know you matter; your life is important; you must love yourself in word and deed. Let's talk about some steps to ensure that everything you do from now on supports the statement: "The rest of my life will be the best of my life."

The first thing you must do is acknowledge the importance of loving you and know you have the ability to create and live the life you were born to live.

Ask yourself, "How can I experience "No Ordinary Love" in my life?"

- Admit where you. What is your current status?
- Have a conversation with yourself about where you want to be.
- Make a commitment to be a part of your own rescue.
- Believe you have the right to love and be loved.

- Change your mindset and thinking.
- Be willing to support and encourage yourself.
- Accept your past and the not-so-good choices you have made throughout life.
- Believe that your past has created some awesome lessons and opportunities for you today.
- Know your purpose (what you love to do, what is your passion, etc.).
- Make daily affirmations that support your purpose.
- Make a list of all of your accomplishments in the last five (5) years and say, "You go girl!" after each one.
- Look in the mirror for the next twenty-one (21) days and say at least five (5) times a day: "I love me!"

As you continue to love yourself, you will not be affected by the choices and decisions others make concerning you. You will understand that what is for you is for you. You will be able to embrace the process of life and count the things in your life that don't work out as being lessons of blessings. Loving you causes you to operate on a different level of thinking, and it allows you to celebrate the good, the bad, the pretty, and the not-so-pretty things in your life.

I commend you for purchasing and reading the information in this book. My intent, along with the other authors, is to encourage you to take action steps after reading each story, each chapter, and/or poem. People often say that knowledge is power, but I believe what you do with the knowledge you receive becomes power. So I strongly encourage you to follow through, take action steps, and begin living the life you were created to live. Purpose is all over you, and there is a story in you that is waiting to touch someone's life, but you must begin to engulf your life, in and with love, so you can be effective in touching the lives of others. "No Ordinary Love" empowers, strengthens, and opens your eyes to a life of possibilities because you begin to believe that loving you is not selfish, but it is a necessity for you to live.

You are NOW READY to experience a life full of love and purpose. You are NOW READY to give love and command love in your life. NOW ask yourself the question: "How do I love me? Let me count the ways!" NOW begin loving you, your life, your purpose, and everything connected to you. You have NOW experienced "NO ORDINARY LOVE!" Declare and decree: "I love me some me, and I will also honor myself by caring for me and making myself priority in my life!" Let your living begin . . . NOW!

# About Marcella D. Moore
## (CellaD motivates)

Marcella Denise Moore, affectionately known as "Cella D" has been inspiring and empowering women for more than two decades. Ms. Moore is passionate about inspiring, motivating and empowering individuals to discover their authentic selves. She serves as a life-giver of hope, motivator and exhorter. Her message is one of purpose, destiny, self-love and strength. Cella D's messages encourages her audience to embrace the process of life, as the lessons life are designed to empower, ignite, activate and release your best self.

Currently she is the facilitator of the weekly Motivate and Pray conference call; a call she founded that is dedicated to motivation, inspiration and prayer; the monthly "Caring for the Caregiver" support call; co-host of the "Be You" show and organizer of the semi-annual "Ladies Night Out" that brings women together for an evening of networking and empowerment.

For the last fifteen years Marcella has worked as Director of Grants at Legal Services of New Jersey. In this position she manages all facets of state-wide grants for New Jersey legal services' programs.

Cella D is a member of Abundant Life Worship Church in New Brunswick, NJ, where she serves on the Special Events Ministry and is one of the facilitators for the daily corporate prayer call. She also serves as a moderator and speaker for conferences, workshops, conference calls and she is a domestic violence response team member for the local police department and women's awareness organization.

Marcella is passionate about her work and her family. She embraces her single-parent status and is the proud mother of her two adult children daughter, Jessteni and son, Elisha. Ms. Moore is a graduate of the Katherine Gibbs Business School, has certifications in Event Management and Paralegal Studies and is a veteran of the United States Army.

Marcella finds comfort in one of her favorite quotes by Marianne Williamson; a quote that sums up her life philosophy quite well. *"Your playing small does not serve the world. There is nothing enlightened about shrinking so that other people won't feel insecure around you. We are all meant to shine, as children do. We were born to make manifest the glory of God that is within us."* Marcella's prayer is that the light of God on her life shines bright enough to make babies leap, hearts open and sleeping giants awake.

# MASTERPIECE
## By: Desh Dixon

I know we've been programmed
To always fear the unknown
I know most of us have gifts and talents
That have yet to be shown.
I know sometimes you wonder
Why you're here, why you were born
I know many of us have been through so much
Some of us fall in the category of a woman scorned.
When you look into the mirror
You are disappointed with what you see
You cry and tear yourself down
Sometimes disgusted, you ask yourself, what happened to me?
You've been broken, hurt, and abused
After you trusted those closest to you.
The stories are all the same
No matter your color, gender or race
Ladies, it's time to reclaim your value
It's time to click erase.
Everyone goes through struggle
Everyone experiences strife
What doesn't kill you only makes you stronger
Trust and believe, no one has a perfect life.
Learn to forgive those that hurt you
So you can take back your power
Let the past go and start to move forward
No more drowning in sorrow or cower.

> You are a beautiful child of God
> No matter your past mistakes
> Have faith that it will all work out
> With God's help, you will never break.
> You are strong, loving and kind
> You are blessed and don't forget fine.
> There is nothing you can't do
> But first you have to believe
> Believe in yourself and know you are worthy
> You are the chief of your magnificent dreams.
> Take a stand for who you are
> Stand in your truth and be in peace
> No more bondage, no more limiting beliefs
> Just walking tall, head up with ease.
> You are not tainted, you are a masterpiece.

Tuesday, October 28, 2014

Ladies, you are beautiful.

Every blemish, every scar, every freckle – you are beautiful! You are enough. You are more than enough. We're constantly bombarded with society's definition of beauty. We face rejections in our lives for the color of our skin, for being too fat, for being too skinny, and so forth. Perfection doesn't exist. You are perfectly imperfect. God made you unique. There is no one like you. Embrace who you are. The right people will love you for who you are.

Ladies, we are doing it all today. I'm so proud of how far we've come. We're strong and can handle a lot of things that come our way. One thing that is important for women to do is to find a balance. Part of being balanced means taking time out for yourself. I don't think we show ourselves as much love as we should. Loving yourself is number one. Not having a healthy relationship with yourself can negatively affect you in many areas of your life. Self-respect and self-love are a must.

Ladies, stop settling. You deserve the very best that life has to offer. When it comes to relationships, a relationship is supposed to enhance or complement your life, not subtract from it. Being in a relationship where you are not growing is unhealthy. Unhealthy meaning not good for your spirit and soul. God didn't create you to be mediocre. He blessed you with gifts and talents that you need to share with the world, to fulfill your purpose. Trust your intuition, trust your gut instincts. Please love yourself enough to walk away from anyone or anything that no longer serves you. If you're being abused or you're not happy or if you're just going through the motions because it's familiar, let it go! You deserve so much more. Love yourself. When you show yourself love, you'll attract that energy of love back to you. I know you may get lonely from time to time but you are worth it. Give more to yourself. I know from experience that the sun is always shining behind the clouds. We just have to have faith and pay attention to what God is trying to reveal to us. I use the term God but you may call it something different. Your higher power, source, divine, mother nature – just trust in that to guide you. God loves you. Trust God will bring someone to you that will be in harmony and alignment with your vision. Until then, be peacefully single.

With Love and Peace,
Desh

# About Desh Dixon

Radesha "Desh" Dixon is a former beauty queen. She is an entrepreneur, speaker, author, and poet on the rise, passionate about empowering others to live their best life. A few of her past pageant titles include Miss Virginia Petite, Miss VA Sunburst Overall, and Miss Virginia Petite East Coast USA. She has also been a cover model finalist for Supermodels Magazine.

Desh obtained her MBA from Strayer University and her Bachelor's degree in Mass Communications from Virginia Commonwealth University. She was a previous member of Toastmasters. She was featured on Dr. Joe Vitale's, 'The Secret Mirror' and 'The Secret Reflection'. She has always had a passion for writing ever since she was younger. She won writing awards in school. Her poems have been in anthologies. One of her poems received 'Honorable Mention' from The National Authors Registry in the Fall 2000 Iliad Literary Awards Program. She likes reading, writing, traveling, listening to music and the performing arts.

Her own life experiences led her on a spiritual self-empowerment journey to rediscover her own purpose. Because of the wisdom and knowledge she has gained, she is on a mission to help others find their own inner power just as she did. She believes that greatness lies within everyone.

She currently resides in the Washington DC metro area.

FOLLOW HER ON FACEBOOK:
https://www.facebook.com/PetiteWithPurpose
https://www.facebook.com/Desh.Dixon

LINK TO HER TWITTER:
https://twitter.com/DeshDixon

LINK TO HER CHANNEL:
https://www.youtube.com/channel/UC9oqgCY2nVt70FlhG-avNPg

Entrepreneur, Author, Speaker, Poetess.

# 3 Excerpts
## By: Rustie McDonald

Carpe La Crap!" Rustie MacDonald, "What is YOUR Fear?"

"The cricket was still clinging to that door at 45 mph! His antennas where straight back and I was feeling guilty but the people behind me would have been rather annoyed if I slowed down. So, 45 MPH and Jiminy, my new friend, hung on for dear life. Antennae's where flat against his head and he made it the 7 miles to Starbucks. Then he hopped off and has never returned.

What amazed me was the shear determination of his quest. Why on earth did this cricket want to hang on for dear life? Determination?" Rustie MacDonald, "The Cricket who Road to Starbucks"

"So, I am really…really….old..

I mean cute…….

Funny as hell and a terrific cook with incredible long legs! Yes, all of these things and more! I am brilliantly gifted at pulling when the door says "push" and taking a left when I should take a right. I am 40 lbs over my preferred weight and I enjoy hitting the snooze button on my phone. I am rarely ever late but often overwhelmed. I say YES when I should say no and I am easily the "helper" when I am the one who actually needs help! I inquire often and want to question everything. I believe in Justice and find the very idea that justice fails so many people-including my family- incomprehensible." Rustie MacDonald, "Get up. Get REAL. Get Happy"

"I have learned that I have nothing to lose. I have everything to gain. I accept my human experience for what it is. I accept that I do not know any "thing" or at least allow my "sh-ego" something and I ll accept that I know some "thing's". I have, since my divorce, accepted that I am a miraculously complex string of crazy DNA and a juicy liquid sack of squeezable love and tenderness. I am a delicious, delightful smile at most, and at the very least I have jokes! I am not a master or a guru. I am a human going through stuff. The stuff I like to call "Lessons". However, I can tell you very honestly before my healing journey, I would call "Lessons" a whole pile of shit.

Crap!!!

Shit Crap!

Crappy Shit!

# About Rustie MacDonald

Rustie MacDonald is an Author, Life Coach, Single Mother, Blogger, Celiac, Motivational Speaker and International Radio Talk Show Host.

# P.R.O.
# (Pushing Resilience Over)

By: Serena Dorsey

We all have the ability to be a P.R.O. Being a P.R.O. does not mean obtaining perfection but essentially learning to Push Resilience Over by taking your growth step by step. At some point in our life we must find something worth striving for. Often reflecting on a favorite song, quote, or prayer can potentially be the "pick me up" needed to give us the motivation to try again tomorrow. Hope for today and trust your future. Do not give up! Believe in progress; not perfection. I share with you my expression of determination, admiration, and belief in one's self; and I hope it assist you in becoming a P.R.O. in your life.

## (Pushing)

**P-Passion, Persistence, Possibilities, Proactive, Participate…**

Passions are a road map to fulfillment. Narrow down your passions in life, and provide focus directly to each individual passion. Do not chase someone else's dream or image of what you should become. Learn to ignore the whispers of naysayers and doubters around you. Unfortunately, often whisperers are persons that are within your circle. You must begin creating a circle of encouragement and empowerment even through your failures. Failing is a process of growth and allowing the process can lead to your ultimate success…

Be persistent in your dreams and goals even when your vision is wavy. Tweaking may be necessary along the way, but no matter what; you do not stop! You do not give up! Do not dwell on steps you stumble on, do not give energy to fear, and do not believe impossibilities.

Possibilities in my terms are defined as, proposed options in future results. Many options will be proposed to you; which ones deserve your faith? Do you put faith in the process of failure or do you put in faith in the process of succeeding? What would happen if you put faith in the possibility of growing past your circumstance?

Proactive keeps you moving towards your goal despite the walls that seem unclimbable. Remaining proactive can help you eliminate moments of being reactive to situations. So many times we shy away from an opportunity because we are simply not prepared. We develop bad habits of preparing at the outcome rather than making preparation part of the process. Allowing procrastination to stay at the foundation of your process could cause you to miss out on growth and development.

Participate in your goals and dreams. Never sit on the sideline and wait for things to fall in place because most likely they won't. Your vision, your goal, your work… Find your passion; believe in the possibility, remain persistent, be proactive toward your goal, and participate in the plan.

## (Resilience)

### R-Repress, Resilient, Rejuvenate, Recognition, Reverence …

Repress your own negative thoughts and the negative thoughts of others. Each day find a positive quote that resonates with your heart and soul. Hang it somewhere you frequent each day. Read it out loud often and no matter how silly you sound keep doing it. Make a habit of feeding something positive each day to your mind, body, and spirit.

Resilience equals survival. Be resilient in your efforts. For each no you receive, consider what could have it made it a yes. Try a different route, prepare a different way, and filter your dreams through a different vision. Accept your fall backs as lessons and not defeat. Learn from the lesson and continue to seek your dream.

Rejuvenate your mind, body, and soul. Learn ways to rejuvenate yourself and give yourself permission to do so. It is easy to become exhausted in our efforts but you cannot let it stop you. You allow yourself to reboot, and recharge all the awesomeness you were destined to give. You and the many that cannot wait to receive your gift will greatly appreciate it.

Recognize the progress you've made thus far. Your journey may seem long ahead, but you are not where you started. It is okay to recognize it and reward yourself for doing so. Giving yourself kudos will help you reflect on what you have accomplished and where you want to go next.

Reverence equates to attention and dedication. When you truly respect something in your life, you tend to make it important and give attention. Have reverence for your dream; give your vision the credit it deserves. Just as you refuse to allow someone to disrespect someone or something dear to you; it is the same way with your dreams. Never allow someone to disrespect or down play your goals; just because they do not understand or relate to them does not mean they have the right to disregard you or your thoughts. Make your thoughts, dreams, and goals a priority.

## (Over)

### O-Obedient, Optimistic, Overzealous, Outgoing, Outstanding

Obedience can equate to abundance. Many times we have "a million" ideas and some may say they can get it all done due to being great at multi-tasking; however, some things require more dedication and attention in order for them to truly be awesome. Therefore, be obedient to your task. Give it the energy and focus it deserves to blossom into its greatest capacity. Once you've allowed it to bloom; feed it, water it, and then move on to planting new seeds. Master your dream and keep dreaming.

Be optimistic! There will always be the fear of the unknown; the "what if", and the "could be". Yet, instead of asking; what if it doesn't work? Or, thinking; this could be a failure. Be optimistic; change your mindset with thoughts such as, this will be a success, this will be amazing? Change your wording and your thoughts. You will be surprised at how your outlook changes as well. Overzealous behavior is not prideful when it comes to your success. Absolutely, positively be overzealous in your pursuit for success. There is nothing too great if your mind produced it; it is achievable. You have permission to have the audacity to be successful and pursue your success.

Outgoing persons are imperfect people with fears, but also hold a vision to triumph obstacles that come their way. Be outgoing in your pursuit of success and set time aside each day toward that pursuit.

Outstanding qualities live within every person. No matter who said you weren't or what failure made you feel you were less than, know that you are outstanding and the gift you can provide to the world is outstanding as well.

Become a P.R.O. from where you are in your life at this moment. There is no perfect day or time to begin pursuing your purpose. The more you pull away from it, the more you will find yourself consistently feeling unfulfilled. Participate in being proactive about your passion and be persistent in your possibilities. Give yourself recognition for what you've achieved thus far and rejuvenate yourself throughout your journey. Be resilient in your process and repress the negative blocks that will flow your way; have reverence for what you can bring forward. You have permission to be overzealous and outgoing to your passions. You are an outstanding quality of purpose and you must be obedient to that purpose. Remain optimistic and believe that despite all odds what you desire can manifest. Take time to develop qualities of a P.R.O. in your life, have the audacity to believe in your dreams. I wish honest fruits of blessings and love as you grow and gain strength in Pushing Resilience Over.

# About Serena Dorsey

Serena N. Dorsey is a Mother, Author, Entrepreneur and Motivator born in Washington, DC and raised in the surrounding DMV area. Since the age of nine, Serena has been writing short stories and poems, and has always imagined her words could inspire and uplift; but allowed her passions to fizzle. In 2013 Serena decided to follow her heart despite fears and leave her financial career of 8 years to begin putting more time and energy into her passions. After devoting time to discovering her passions, Serena took a leap of faith in 2014 and submitted her first published work "Me" featured in the Best Seller Poets Against Bullying. Serena is presently developing her most exciting project to date that is geared toward helping people believe and accomplish one dream at a time.

*"Dreams are a beautiful start to success." ~Serena N. Dorsey*

Serena holds many titles yet breathes a strong passion for family and is proud of being the youngest of four siblings, the mother of a beautiful, intelligent daughter, and Aunt of 13 nieces and nephews. Serena looks forward to continuing to grow her passions and helping many others find theirs. She also has two books in the working to be published respectively in 2015.

# HER
## By: Sorena Eaddy

Shattered
Shattered
Another broken heart
Ripped at the core
Cause see she met him and he met her
Perfect they thought they would be
He was nothing like what she was use to
And she was all the good that he needed
Oh but time changes things
He did not connect
And she couldn't come correct
No future
No plans
Just playing until they felt like the plane has landed
Characteristics burst at the seam
Lies, deceit, and all ugly things
How could Mr. Perfect, her dream, be a nightmare
See she had daddy issues and so did he
Looking to fill voids where hurt lingered for so long
Never really knowing how to love each other
Pouring into one another all the garbage and junk that built over the years
Setting expectations that neither one of them could meet
But then one day a sign appeared
He left so suddenly without a trace

She pleaded she begged
He held his head in disgrace
He couldn't tell her he didn't know how to love her
He couldn't tell her that he was still hurting from past mistakes
He couldn't tell her that he was afraid
He couldn't tell her that this was a risk he did not want to take.
So anger and bitterness carried on in her
She cried out to God "Why me?"
But he did not response
She waited patiently
Then as gentle as the wind He spoke
Daughter I am all you need
Cling to me and love me
I have created you for wonderful things
I just need you to make yourself available
You were caught up things, people, and situations
You forgot about me
I need you
You are my messenger
So that's when she met Him again
Only this time it was perfect
Because he made her whole
Filled those empty spots

**He showed her "Her"**

# About Sorena Eaddy

Sorena Eaddy, a native of Wilmington, Delaware, is an author, inspirational speaker, and minister in training. Sorena shares her love of service in the community by volunteering with various youth groups and mentoring young women. She is an instrument in spreading the good news about Christ to young people and helping them transform their lives for the Kingdom of God. She believes you're never too young, or too old, to live for Christ.

# I Am Beautiful

## By: Vanessa J. Ross

I am beautiful,
because God made me.

I am strong,
because my strength comes from God to share with others.

I am courageous,
because this is how God wants me to be.

I am beautiful,
I am strong;
just one look in the mirror tells it all.

I Am Beautiful!!!!

# Convict Lover
## By: Terri Melissa Campbell

Appeared so sweet
I rationalized…
there's good within us all

Sold
upon this idea
That "love"
could change the small

Beneath the warmth
to my surprise
A bed
of poison quills

Upon his chest
I pressed my ears
I hear
the anger shrill

Like seashells echo back the shore
I stood
traumatized

Heard
Sweeping waves
of tidal rage

Hate
glistened through the eyes

I should've
ran
without goodbye
before
it was too late

How was I to know
that
brute
was there
innate

Apology roses
sent to me
my blood
the thorns did splatter

Above my grave
etched in stone
the emblem of the battered

Women, we are the nurturers and givers of society. We give and give and give and sometimes with no return or reward. Women are strong yet vulnerable, soft yet granite-like. Women are the core of family and the movement of people's lives other than their own. In the midst of daily decisions and responsibilities there is a loyalty to the ones we love whether spouses, children or parents. The only problem with our relentless loyalty is the lack of placing ourselves first.

There some women who find themselves in negative situations where they are not only taken for granted but also treated less than humane.

These women who struggle with domestic violence are placed in such a difficult position where their homes become virtual prisons. For a woman to be a giver of love, affection and care and in return receive the blunt force of a fist is devastation without words. There are only the groans of the soul and the torment of not knowing if she will survive to see another day. The very arms that once were wrapped around her body in passion and pleasure are the same arms that hammer down to beat, hurt and destroy her. The internal conflict of emotion that she must face becomes a weight of despair on her heart.

There is never a moment that it is okay for a woman to feel threatened in or out of her home, especially by anyone who she is in a relationship with. Mistreatment is never acceptable. It is never warranted and most importantly never deserved. It is important to understand that violence begets violence so women must also refrain from striking a man. Any form of abuse whether verbal, physical or emotional is not a characteristic of love. Love is not a jacket you can wear that one takes off and puts on when ready. Love doesn't hurt. Love is not disrespect. Love is not optional in a relationship. In I Corinthians 13:4-5 (NLT) of the Bible, it explains that "love is patient and kind. Love is not jealous, boastful, proud or rude. It does not demand its own way. It is not irritable, and it keeps no record of being wronged". So when an abuser apologizes time and time again and says the words, "I love you" please understand there is a true definition of the word "love". Understanding what love truly is will be manifested through actions and not simply words.

Women are created beautiful, embrace your potential and celebrate the special gift of uniqueness that God created as "you". It is never your fault someone lacks self-control. It is never your fault that your abuser devalues womanhood and treats you as disposable. The abuser's character flaws and internal ugliness is not a reflection of the woman you are. However in the midst of all the turmoil, our strength is formed in weakness. The process of going through something traumatic becomes a beam of light. That light illuminates a bad situation and becomes the teaching moment. It teaches the lesson that you are worth more; worth being cherished, protected, and valued .

If there is a glimmer of hope for those trapped in this situation, it is the fact YOU ARE NOT ALONE. There are people who care and other women who have successfully come out of unhealthy, dangerous relationships. There are organizations, churches, and survivors who are ready, willing and able to help. It is imperative if you or someone you know are suffering in silence, please contact the National Domestic Violence Hotline at 1-800-799-SAFE (7233). There is hope, there is help and most importantly there is you. You deserve to be truly loved.

# About Terri Melissa Campbell

Terri M. Dunkley-Campbell resides in Westchester County, NY with her husband Alfred Jr., three children, Austin, Asia, Alina and her beloved dog, Teddie. She has two stepdaughters, Charine and Lauren who reside in New Jersey. She graduated from Elizabeth Seton College with a degree in business administration, and continued her education in nursing, and insurance. As a pianist, her love of music lead her to start CetaPepper Publishing in 2007 to house her writings, catalog of compositions, lyrics, produce and arrange music, as well as manage up and coming artists. As a singer-songwriter she worked over the years with Zerohour Music, Bellyhouse Records, GraceFull Tunes, and Yellow Brick Road Productions and performed as a background singer. She received an award for Cambridge Who's Who in Songwriting, and is the author of the book, "The Absorbent Soul" a collection of poetry and babblings and also a co-author in "HerSpectives"How I Created Work Life Balance". She has most recently started "The Sonnet 27 Project" which serves as a hub for charities. The motto for the project is "Giving Seeds serve Living Needs" where you give up something minor to help others who are in need. She is a licensed nurse and spends her spare time working at a nursing home to care for the elderly. Her mission is to continue on with her music ministry, to inspire others to be compassionate, and to be a force for positive change.

www.cetapepper.com　　　　　　　　　　twitter: @CetaPepper
www.sonnet27.com　　　　　　　　email: tm1vision@optonline.net

# Tainted Elegance – My Story
### By: Terri LaPoint

Most of us like the idea of a fairy tale life, living happily ever after. But what we tend to forget is that every fairy tale begins with a dark side. Before the damsel in distress can be rescued by the knight in shining armor, there is first the distress from which she must be rescued. There is a wicked witch or a horrible dragon that has imprisoned her or stolen her voice. At the root of every fairy tale is a lie, told by an evil villain trying to steal the voice, the destiny, the identity, and even the very life of the central character. Victory comes as she learns the truth, finds her voice, and steps into her destiny, which happens as the good Prince rides in on his valiant steed and defeats the villain, freeing her to be who she was born to be.

My own tale began with an attempt on my life in the womb. I miraculously survived an abortion procedure that resulted in the death of my twin sister. It has been almost three years since I learned the shocking truth that left me reeling, but explained everything. That truth has changed me, defined me, and awakened in me a passion like never before to be a voice for the voiceless.

There was a time in my life that I was timid and afraid. I wanted desperately to matter, but I was too afraid to step out. Not any more. I have survived something that few live to tell about, and now I have the amazing opportunity to speak out for others whose voices are being silenced through writing their stories in my job as an investigative reporter. If I didn't know my story, I wouldn't have the courage to do what I do now.

My mother didn't know that she was carrying twins when she went to have the abortion. She was around 14 weeks along. My twin sister and I loved each other as only twins sharing the same womb can do. Her name is Leanne. We had to have sensed that something was wrong. There were flashes of light and stainless steel as the instruments came in to the place that had once been warm and secure. Like strobe lights in the darkness – the stuff of my nightmares. Leanne was first, and she literally kicked and shoved me with her tiny body to the top of the womb, giving me a chance to live. She was ripped apart, and then, there was only silence. I was alone, and rejected by my own mother. It was only later that she would learn that she was still pregnant, but circumstances prevented her from finishing the job.

God hid me, and I survived, thanks to the selflessness of a tiny person thought too small to make a difference. She made all the difference in the world. Her voice was silenced, but mine was not.

My name is Terri LaPoint and I am an abortion survivor.

# About Terri LaPoint

Terri LaPoint is a writer, speaker, childbirth and breastfeeding educator, doula, and assistant midwife. She writes for PolitiChicks and Health Impact News, investigating stories of Medical Kidnappings. She has also written for the Inquisitr and Midwifery Today, and has spoken at several Trust Birth Conferences. She holds a B.S. in Cultural Anthropology/World Missions with minors in Bible & Theology, and Behavioral Science from Toccoa Falls College. She is a homeschool mom and a passionate defender of life, truth, and freedom, as well as a voice for the voiceless.

# Love Is My Superpower
## By: Toy Parker

When it comes to love, I am the one who gives their all. Every. Single. Time. No. Matter. What. Literally, it doesn't matter what area of life I engage in, I don't know how to not put my all into it. There are no in-betweens for me. I'm all in or I'm all out. That's just the way I am wired. In one relationship, I was once gave my all to the point where not only did I not have anything left to give, but I had lost myself in the process of doing the one thing I knew in my heart I did the best above all my skills and many talents: love.

I never ever, EVER, thought I'd ever in a million years quote R&B singer and former New Edition member, Bobby Brown, but he said something during an interview while reflecting on the death of his ex-wife, Whitney Houston that I could definitely relate to. He said, "Sometimes, we, you know, love a person so hard that we're loving them wrong, and maybe I did that." Looking back, Bobby, maybe I did that too. It appears he learned a valuable lesson in love. I must admit, I did too.

I spent two decades of my life loving the same guy. That's a long time, right?! I know. If it's any consolation, I met him when I was a child. So it started when I was 7 and he was 5, about to turn 6. This little boy ran to my father, who was the assistant principal of our school at the time who everyone was afraid of (my ex-husband's father was a teacher at the same school) and this brave little boy, pulled on my Dad's pant leg and asked him could he sit with me in his office while I waited for my Dad afterschool every day. He gave him permission and the rest was history.

We talked everyday about every and anything. I really liked him and we were the best of friends. True friends in every sense of the word.

We got older and after middle school he moved to a neighboring school and we still stayed in touch. Then came high school and he was my first date to the prom. Then came dating. And breaking up. And dating again. And breaking up and falling madly in love with each other all over again. A cycle of forgiving and moving on and going back to what was so very familiar and what in the craziest of ways felt like home. Then came college and him leaving his hoop dreams behind to follow me to college while he was dating someone else. I was by this time showing early but prominent signs of a workaholic as I was involved in campus organizations and working in the media industry as an undergraduate pursuing my passion in broadcasting after turning down a full engineering scholarship. Yes, that's a story for another time. Back to the subject of love.

By the time we were in our 20s, he was still known as the ladies' man and I was still known as the good girl, the original goal digger, and the one who was wife material. He knew that, and despite his raging hormones, he always would come running back to me to tell me how he knew I was who he wanted and how he would make me his once and for all. What woman wouldn't want to hear that? Promises. Promises. Promises. In spite of it all, I always believed. Then the decade came where reality just couldn't live up to the dream.

He had always wanted to marry me to have his child. So when I found out he had gotten someone pregnant and had decided to marry them, my whole world stopped. I was so devastated in the midst of all my accomplishments and accolades. Nothing else mattered in that one moment. All that mattered was that somehow he broke his promises to me. He told me crying over the phone, apologizing. I couldn't hear anything. My life as far as I knew it was over. Quite an illogical assessment but when you love someone to the point of no return, that's what happens. At that time I was a bit feisty so I told him, "You made your bed now you can lie in it." I meant that literally and figuratively and he knew that for sure. By the grace of God, I pulled myself back together again and moved on—again.

No matter what he would still always come back. Was that love? He would always say how much he loved me. How he never felt so strong for anyone else before in all his life. I understood that feeling. I felt that feeling too but now life is complicated. He's married with a child and I have real choices to make. I told him I am not going to hell for anybody. Love or no love. Even while he's telling me how he's so hurt because he was cheated on. The irony, right? There's so much that happened in between that. Me getting him out of trouble with the law due to his alcoholism that triggered after the death of his father that I totally underestimated the depths of or my usual miracle work I'd do on his behalf because I loved him so very much. Then the day came when I told him there's nothing else to discuss until he has divorce papers and how we could never be under any other circumstances.

Then the day came years later when he called to tell me he was divorced and he wanted us to start again and this time date to marry. I was speechless because he finally chose me. By this time, I'm in my late 20s, still not married, no child, and still not over him. I had plenty of options of really great and stable men who wanted to date me. My ex-husband was the exception to all of my rules regarding dating and marrying a man. When that curly headed-bright eyed man looked me into my eyes, I lost my mind. I would remember the decades of laughter, love and more love and the memories of the feeling when I was in his arms. Jesus wept. I was weak for him. Everyone warned me not to go back to him and how it would bring my life down. My desire and love for him defied all points of reason. I dated him anyway and there were many ups, quite a few downs, a marriage, a baby and – abandonment.

Yep, the alcoholism got the best of him and he let that contribute to the demise of the marriage. My workaholic coping mechanism didn't help the situation either. After a blissful marriage and much consummation of the marriage that finally happened, he went on a drinking binge and left me during my third month of pregnancy. It took all the love I had within me to not succumb to depression and carry our daughter almost to term and deliver her a month early during 51 ½ hours of labor and no husband present. We tried to reconcile after she was born but I told him I refuse to raise her in an alcoholic home and that he needed to get treatment in order to return to the home. He chose alcohol and the lifestyle that comes with that over his new family. To this day, he always apologizes for the hell he put me through before, during and after the marriage as we've been divorced now almost 10 years.

The thing about it is that I carried that same dysfunctional behavior into my work environment and in other relationships with potential mates and even family members and would endure for the sake of love until one day I woke up. I stopped making people, my ex-husband included, the exception to my rules regarding giving and showing me the respect I deserve the day I remembered how exceptional I am in Jesus Christ.

There was a time when I was younger I often thought of my love as a weakness. I didn't always feel that way. So many would say to me, "You're so nice". "You'll get run over in relationships because you are so loving". "How can you be so forgiving?" "Men will take your kindness for weakness." "You could never make it in corporate – you're just too nice." There were times I actually subscribed to these notions, especially after experiencing pain during my on again- off again relationship with my now ex-husband as aforementioned that almost spanned two decades before we even got married. And there were times during my time in corporate where I thought to myself, "What if they are right?" Who wouldn't, right? But fortunately, there was this resounding voice within that would always say, "What if they are all wrong."

When I went inward and took my love that I gave to everyone else and gave it back to myself—something shifted within. That was when I came to understand that love is my superpower. I was not weak to love so hard and unconditionally in any of those circumstances. I was an example of true love that brought everyone closer to the love of God. Therefore, my labor in love was never in vain. Neither is yours, my friend. You were strong and very courageous. I was courageous too but now I'm wiser and realize that I cannot love anyone but to the same degree that I love myself. I am in love under new management at this point in my life. The shift that needed to happen in my life was inside of me. People treat me differently now because of the way I treat myself.

What's happening outside is only a reflection of what's happening inside of me. I am growing in love. I am maturing in love. I am living in love. Love is my superpower and permeates throughout everything I do and everyone I come in contact with. I had to ignite my life from the inside out. My chapter is designed to #IGNITEyourLife today. I had to learn that I deserved to receive love just as much as I love to give it. The same goes for each of you reading this chapter today. When I came to that realization, my whole life opened up. I invite you to allow yours to do the same. Life happens all the time. The question is what are you going to do when it does. I submit to you to live love daily and make love your superpower. It all starts with you.

My ex-husband still pops back into my life from time to time to share his love for me and how he wants to make it right. I have forgiven him so I could truly move on with my life and receive the love I know I deserve for myself and our daughter who deserves to have an active father in her life as she was the fruit from the marriage that did not last half as long as the "romance" or the fairy-tale turned reality-tale. I am grateful that I can extend love toward him without the dysfunction of it all. He knows I love him but can never be with him again in this lifetime. He had his chance many, many times over. For the rest of my life, I choose me.

My love for myself will take me into the relationship that is designed to last the rest of my life. I will let love lead the way this time. God is love.

He works all things together for the good of them who love Him. I had to go through what I went through and breakthrough in love so you can do the same. I had to go inward and soar and #IGNITEyourLife so you can see how love does conquer all and truly covers a multitude of sins. I am loving myself the right way so I can love others the right way. I have gotten rid of toxic relationships and I have replaced them with healthy and thriving ones. It isn't always easy but the journey to self-love is well worth the reward it yields. I trust God more than ever before. He is writing my love story right now even as you are reading this. Because I trust Him, I know I will always have the victory in all areas of my life so that's why I keep loving anyway no matter what. That's why **Love Is My Superpower.**

© *Copyright 2015 Toy Parker*

# About Toy Parker

Toy Parker of www.toyparker.com, is a Modelpreneur, Empowerment Speaker, Creative Content, Marketing and Media Strategist who was named one of the top Media Professionals of 2014. She is a former North Carolina spokesmodel for Covergirl, Oil of Olay, Cadillac and other reputable companies. Toy currently ignites the lives of audiences globally as an emcee, radio, and television host while on the speaking circuit against all odds with a determination to thrive no matter what life brings her way.

Her work over her past 20 years in broadcasting while in the mist of instances of racism, sexism, and even ageism, has been featured on The Word Network, FOX, CBS, ABC, and various radio stations around the world just to name a few. Additionally, Toy's corporate materials created on diversity within the healthcare industry have been featured in publications for Cigna. Her sales and marketing materials created for Hendrick Automotive Group are still used to date for Hendrick Buick Cadillac and GMC.

Toy is a professional level public speaker with 20 plus years experience in empowering audiences in cities, universities, corporations, churches and groups of all sizes. By the grace of God, her *#IGNITEyourLife* platform has also expanded to include a Radio and Television Network that has a worldwide audience of listeners and viewers.

Through her platform, Toy empowers and teaches how to breakthrough life's challenges in relationships and business with love to get the success you desire and deserve! Love is truly her superpower as she #LiveLOVEDaily using what she calls #TheLoveFactor!

Look for this multifaceted and dynamic author's new book releases *#IGNITEyourLife: Ultimate Sparks for a 30 Day Breakthrough* and *Chronicles of a Tween Mom: Fashionista Adventures* on Amazon soon in the months to come!

# My Angel Watching Over Me

### By: Vanessa J. Ross

As I lay asleep meditating on what life is supposed to be,

I look up to you with a smile upon my face, how wonderful is that

My Angel watching over me-

You gave me the strength and courage to go on
when I thought there was nowhere to turn

You are my Angel watching over me

That beautiful smile upon your face lets me
know you're always by my side

My Angel watching over me!

# A Letter to 14 Year Old Yvette

*By: Yvette Jordan*

I have often wondered..If I had the chance to talk to the 14 Year old me.. What would I say to her? I chose 14 because that was the age when life became different for me..1983 was a life changing!! I realized by my 14th Birthday that I had a voice...not an ordinary voice..but an Extraordinary voice!! I found that I was blessed with the gift of song and that I was also blessed with a beautiful way of allowing the the words that flowed from my heart..to come to alive on paper...The very things I longed for my mouth to be able to speak...I could write ...that not only warmed my heart or gave me a private platform in which I found the utmost freedom..but that it also created a very special place that belonged only to myself..A place to go when refuge was needed..where I felt the wind in my wild hair..So i felt with the all the trials and tribulations that My eyes have seen thus far..I would tell My young Yvette these words:

Yvette..

Today starts a different version and journey of LIFE I was Blessed to be able to come back to teach you how to survive..

On our 14th birthday you experienced something new.

Little did I know..throughout your life..it will become very useful to you

All of the "grown up" conversations you indulged in with the True Divas I hope was inhaled for inspiration

This journey you are about to embark is going to require your full
attention and your ability to learn random forms of education
I don't want to scare you ..I just need to make you aware

A completely different type of life from what
you are familiar awaits you out there

The First thing I want to share..GOD is
wth you at all times..Everywhere

The very best friend you can ever have ..when
you need him..He's always there

The creation and design..GOD made in YOU
unmatched to another ..unique by his divine design..true!!!

God made everyone and everything Beautiful,
Yet there will be people who will not have
the same thought process as you

Those will be the times..you will be tested..
you will need prayer to endure the mess
Yet utilizing the tools lain before you will bring
about your best and navigate your success

Everything is not point blank given..for some
answers you will have to search
It will be worth the findings. when you read
GOD's word and put in the work

Now everything you need to know will now
bring about a smile to your face
However ...there will be an abundance of
smiles at the right time and place

You will need to grow a little thick skin to protect your heart
If not..constantly it will be torn apart

The beauty of having the opportunity to pass through this life
is the joy of wondering what awaits you in paradise
So while you walk this journey..know that GOD is always by your side

He will turn your trials into triumphs
As sure as he waiting to receive you..with his arms stretched out wide!!!

# About Yvette Jordan

My Name is Yvette Denise Jordan

I am The Founder/CEO of 2nd Wynd Entertainment. I am a singer, poet and lyric writer for songs.

I was born and raised in New York City and have had growth of wisdom and knowledge of life challenges and changes in Baltimore, Maryland ,Ft Wayne Indiana and My current home of Lumberton, North Carolina. I bring my experiences of love and life into my work to help as well as be a blessing to others.

# How I Learned To Love My Body – "Imperfections" and All

*By: Nicole Eastman*

Do you struggle with accepting your body?

It starts early, doesn't it?

> *The societal influence.*
> *The comparisons.*
> *The fixation on "imperfections".*

**For me, I battled my body from the time I was young.**

**In elementary school**, I developed early and this was the source of teasing and humiliation.

**In middle school**, I was awkward and I felt ugly. Glasses, bad teeth, overweight, and uncomfortable in my own skin…

**In high school**, I was not the popular girl and I was turned down for a school dance.

*Rejected.*

*Not good enough.*

*Not pretty enough…I thought.*

**In college**, I discovered the gym and I found my love for fitness.

I left clerical work to teach group fitness classes, got paid to workout, and I also gained a fit body.

*Triple win!* ☺

**In between undergrad and medical school**, I worked as a certified personal trainer at Lifetime Fitness, I trained to compete in figure competitions, I gained incredible discipline with food, and I also gained **body dysmorphia.**

> **body dysmorphia**
>
> **Body dysmorphic disorder**, also known as **body dysmorphia** or **dysmorphic** syndrome, is a mental illness that involves belief that one's own appearance is unusually defective, while one's thoughts about it are pervasive and intrusive, although the perceived flaw might be nonexistent.
>
> Body dysmorphic disorder - Wikipedia, the free encyclopedia
> en.wikipedia.org/wiki/Body_dysmorphic_disorder   Wikipedia

**In medical school**, I started a program to assist other medical students, faculty, and staff in achieving better health and fitness, I watched my Dad die of a massive stroke at the age of 53 (he had several preventative risk factors and it killed me inside to know that I wasn't able to help him make better choices), I spent hours at the gym in my attempts to "escape from my pain", and I rotated with a plastic surgeon who told me, *"Don't get pregnant, it will destroy your body."*

**In starting residency**, I was so sleep deprived and overworked that I *couldn't keep weight on* my body.

**When I got married**, I looked at my trim body and **still saw imperfection.**

**When I faced my death two weeks following my wedding**, my body experienced **permanent consequences and disability**.

**When I spent over seven months in bed due to pain**, my body yelled at me for being *so ungrateful*.

*Gratitude is the healthiest of all human emotions. The more you express gratitude for what you have, the more likely you will have even more to express gratitude for.*

*Zig Ziglar*

**When I was *blessed* with pregnancy**, I prayed for my body to hold up and for the birth of a healthy baby.

**When my body gained 70 pounds during pregnancy**, my body could barely move.

**When I went into labor**, I did not know if my back would be able to take more trauma.

After hours of labor, my son went into fetal distress.

I remember feeling like I was living a nightmare – I was scared.

I was emotional and I felt disappointed as they **rushed me for an emergency c-section**.

To think I was proud of making it this far with no stretch marks, and now I would end up with a scar.

**Through my son, I gained acceptance of my beauty.
I finally learned to love my body.**

So what changed?

**My BODY changed.**

Through discipline learned years earlier, I chose to make wise **lifestyle choices.**

However, my motivation became much deeper than the superficial appearance I sought out in the past.

Now, my son was my reason to **truly live** and live *as well as I could.*

**Despite losing the pregnancy weight, I have aged** – gracefully, I hope ☺

**Do you embrace your gift of aging?**

**My body has changed and that is okay.**

Underneath, most of us have some sort of scar, don't we?

In addition to a permanent scar, which serves as reminder of the delivery of my healthy child, **my breasts have changed.**

They **fed my son.**

In times of near homelessness, they nourished his body and allowed him to grow and thrive.

In addition to nourishing his body, **breastfeeding nourished my soul.**

**I finally *found confidence in my femininity*** – a side of me I never learned how to embrace prior.

In growing a child, my breasts have lost their youth. This is okay.

What an amazing gift the female body is.

**My MIND changed.**

Rather than choosing to focus on what I could see as an imperfection, I **chose to start looking at each perceived imperfection for its unique sense of beauty.**

What all I would have missed out on had it not been for each of these "perfect imperfections".

Now, tell me what you perceive as an imperfection.

For example, maybe it is the presence of wrinkles?

To me, when I see a body filled with wrinkles, I see a tapestry of beauty.

To think of all of the wonderful memories, the blessing of a relatively long life, and the wisdom gained through the time required to craft such art.

Your mind is powerful.

**Will you do me a favor and recondition your mind, so you can find beauty in all things?**

**My SOUL changed.** Becoming a Mom allowed me to gain greater purpose in life.

In growing through parenting, I have realized just how beautiful the body is.

I believe that in learning to love my body, my son will gain appreciation for true beauty.

I am amazed by the body's capabilities, and life itself.

**Life is a miracle.**

*My mother was the most beautiful woman I ever saw. All I am I owe to my mother. I attribute my success in life to the moral, intellectual, and physical education I received from her."*

*George Washington*

## Nicole Eastman

# The Girl in the Mirror
## By: Wilma Harris

Who's that girl in the mirror?
She has pimples and a few freckles
But, Wow look at that smile.
Now her hair doesn't flow
Like a Next Top Model
But the way she stands so confident
And fierce, says more than hair ever could.
Again, who's that girl I am looking at in the mirror?
That girl is BOLD
That girl is CONFIDENT
That girl has FLAWS
Most of all, that girl is BEAUTIFUL
Whoever she is, I love what I see.
Oh wait, that girl is ME.

# YOU

### By: Ashley Love

Don't be afraid of what they will see.
Dream and be who you want to be.
Don't run from your problems,
Or long on the past.
For If you do, your love for yourself
Will never last.
Don't change for anyone
Or let your dreams fade away
For you will be the one being admired someday.
See yourself as one of a kind
And you inner beauty people will find.
Let your fears disappear as you grow stronger
And your legendary smile will live on for much longer.

# ABC
## By: Takia Smith

First of All, I want to thank My Lord and Savior Jesus Christ for this amazing opportunity. Second Ms. Ashley Love thanks for choosing me to be a part of Tainted Elegance where I have the opportunity to share on the topics of Attitude, Beauty and Confidence.

It is and Honor and a privilege to write this chapter. I dedicate my chapter to my amazing Husband Terrence, and the loves of my life Master Khalil, Sir Terrence and Princess Kamille, My babies I love them to pieces.

I want to share a few tips with you on Attitude Beauty and Confidence. Let's just call it the ABC's on Being Beautiful on the inside and out.

There is a difference between pretty and beautiful. When someone is pretty, they have a good appearance. But when someone is beautiful, they shine on the inside and out.

**Let's just start with Attitude**

Attitude When I speak of attitude, my emotions get real. Have you ever ran into someone and gave them the greeting of the day, Good Morning, Good Day, How are you? And they look at you with a mean mug. That is not the kind of attitude that us women should have. When you are blessed to wake up an additional morning you should be more than honored to speak to your sisters. A word of inspiration to sisters and brothers even if you don't know their name can go a long way. My most favorite greeting of the day is Good Morning my love! When asked "how is my day" It is always wonderful. Why is that you ask, because each day that I can wake up and reach out to at least one more person the last thing that I want to do is push them away by complaining. If it's raining, snowing, thunderstorm, cloudy, or hot, it's still a Wonderful day because I have more moments to bless someone else. So the next time someone that you dont know is even with in hearing distance of you. Shock them by just saying Good Morning!

**Beauty- Ever wanted to see how beautiful you really are?**

Take a few moments to look into the mirror when you first wake up. Take a few moments to be thankful for your breath, beauty and brains. Next let's clean up.

Clean your skin daily! Pick products made for your skin type (oily, dry, combination, normal) in order to achieve the best results. Wash your face no more than two times a day; in the morning and before you go to bed. Be gentle. If you scrub really hard you will only irritate your skin. Skin vigorate cleansing brushes work great. They don't irritate the skin and they can remove up to 85% better than cleaning by hands. Don't ever sleep with your make-up on. Your pores will get clogged and you'll start breaking out. After washing your face, use a good moisturizer that is made for your skin type. If you have blackheads or whiteheads, try using Mary Kay Time wise system.

Keep yourself properly groomed! Wash your hair as often as needed. Use deodorant. Moisturize your skin daily. It's best to do this after you shower because your skin is still damp and the lotion will soak in easily. Grooming your nails is also important. Keep them cut short and buff them once every couple of weeks to keep them smooth and nice. Push back your cuticles to prevent hangnails. Don't ever cut them! If you like nail polish, try using a sheer pink color or clear coat. If you use a sheer pink color, use one coat so the natural color variations of your nails show through. It really does look nice. Mary Kay Satin hands comes in a few different fragrances and it works great as a must have and an amazing home manicure/pedicure ingredient.

Fix up your hair! When getting your hair cut, make sure you know exactly what you want. If you're not sure then ask your hairdresser for a cut that will go with your face shape. You can look up tutorials on curling or straightening your hair on YouTube. Don't spend a ton of time styling your hair. The whole point is to bring out your natural beauty. Find a way to rock your natural style or a style that makes you feel amazing!

Compliment yourself with make-up! Find your favorite facial feature and capitalize it. But don't overdo it, if you go one day without all the makeup everybody will notice and their thoughts won't be very good. If your teeth aren't as white as they could be, don't wear bright lipstick. This will draw attention to the contrast. Instead, for example, wear a dark mascara or eye shadow. This will bring out the beauty of your eyes.

Do one thing for yourself every day! Make yourself do it. It's the ultimate act of self-respect. Soak in the bubble bath or read an inspiring book. These little pleasures allow you to feel special. You can fake it if you need to until you actually feel deserving of it. Whatever you choose, follow the action by writing down what you did and how it made you feel. Make it your own "attitude file". Include stories, quotes from friends and photographs that have made you feel good about yourself.

Feel Good, Feel pretty and that's what the world will see. If you feel ugly that is what people will see. Ensure you feel and look as good as you can. Beauty starts on the inside.

Wow this feels good so awesome to share so jump right in. Confidence. I feel that is another major factor about Beauty!!!!

Self-confidence is the difference between feeling unstoppable and feeling scared out of your wits. Your perception of yourself has an enormous impact on how others perceive you. Perception is reality — the more self-confidence you have, the more likely it is you'll succeed.

Although many of the factors affecting self-confidence are beyond your control, there are a number of things you can consciously do to build self-confidence.

**1. Dress Sharp**

Although clothes don't make the man, they certainly affect the way he feels about himself. No one is more conscious of your physical appearance than you are. When you don't look good, it changes the way you carry yourself and interact with other people. Use this to your advantage by taking care of your personal appearance. In most cases, significant improvements can be made by bathing and shaving frequently, wearing clean clothes, and being cognizant of the latest styles.

This doesn't mean you need to spend a lot on clothes. One great rule to follow is "spend twice as much, buy half as much". Rather than buying a bunch of cheap clothes, buy half as many select, high quality items. In long run this decreases spending because expensive clothes wear out less easily and stay in style longer than cheap clothes. Buying less also helps reduce the clutter in your closet.

**2. Walk Faster**

One of the easiest ways to tell how a person feels about herself is to examine her walk. Is it slow? tired? painful? Or is it energetic and purposeful?

People with confidence walk quickly. They have places to go, people to see, and important work to do. Even if you aren't in a hurry, you can increase your self confidence by putting some pep in your step. Walking 25% faster will make to you look and feel more important.

## 3. Good Posture

Similarly, the way a person carries herself tells a story. People with slumped shoulders and lethargic movements display a lack of self confidence. They aren't enthusiastic about what they're doing and they don't consider themselves important. By practicing good posture, you'll automatically feel more confident. Stand up straight, keep your head up, and make eye contact. You'll make a positive impression on others and instantly feel more alert and empowered.

## 4. Personal Commercial

One of the best ways to build confidence is listening to a motivational speech. Unfortunately, opportunities to listen to a great speaker are few and far between. You can fill this need by creating a personal commercial. Write a 30-60 second speech that highlights your strengths and goals. Then recite it in front of the mirror aloud (or inside your head if you prefer) whenever you need a confidence boost.

## 5. Gratitude

When you focus too much on what you want, the mind creates reasons why you can't have it. This leads you to dwell on your weaknesses. The best way to avoid this is consciously focusing on gratitude. Set aside time each day to mentally list everything you have to be grateful for. Recall your past successes, unique skills, loving relationships, and positive momentum. You'll be amazed how much you have going for you and motivated to take that next step towards success.

## 6. Compliment other people

When we think negatively about ourselves, we often project that feeling on to others in the form of insults and gossip. To break this cycle of negativity, get in the habit of praising other people. Refuse to engage in backstabbing gossip and make an effort to compliment those around you. In the process, you'll become well liked and build self confidence. By looking for the best in others, you indirectly bring out the best in yourself.

## 7. Sit in the front row

In schools, offices, and public assemblies around the world, people constantly strive to sit at the back of the room. Most people prefer the back because they're afraid of being noticed. This reflects a lack of self confidence. By deciding to sit in the front row, you can get over this irrational fear and build your self confidence. You'll also be more visible to the important people talking from the front of the room.

## 8. Speak up

During group discussions many people never speak up because they're afraid that people will judge them for saying something stupid. This fear isn't really justified. Generally, people are much more accepting than we imagine. In fact most people are dealing with the exact same fears. By making an effort to speak up at least once in every group discussion, you'll become a better public speaker, more confident in your own thoughts, and recognized as a leader by your peers.

## 9. Work out

Along the same lines as personal appearance, physical fitness has a huge effect on self confidence. If you're out of shape, you'll feel insecure, unattractive, and less energetic. By working out, you improve your physical appearance, energize yourself, and accomplish something positive. Having the discipline to work out not only makes you feel better, it creates positive momentum that you can build on the rest of the day.

## 10. Focus on contribution

Too often we get caught up in our own desires. We focus too much on ourselves and not enough on the needs of other people. If you stop thinking about yourself and concentrate on the contribution you're making to the rest of the world, you won't worry as much about you own flaws. This will increase self-confidence and allow you to contribute with maximum efficiency. The more you contribute to the world the more you'll be rewarded with personal success and recognition.

By using these 10 strategies you can get the mental edge you need to reach your potential.

I've always been in love with makeup, fashion and anything beauty. I feel like with all these things you can express who you are and it gives you a boost of confidence when you most need it. I decided to write this chapter to teach other woman about the beauty we have inside and out. I also want to share information on all the wonderful products that Mary Kay offers, all dedicated to woman who give so much to others and so little to themselves. Mary Kay focuses on providing the best products to every woman out there because every woman deserves to have the best. That is why I love their products.

Today I wanted to talk about a woman who has inspired me, to not only be the best Mary Kay Consultant possible. She has also inspired me to be the best person that I can be. She has taught me what it is to be brave, what it is to get past all conflicts no matter how hard it may be. To know that you can accomplish anything you put your mind to. How you can get past any ruff situation that you may have or that you had in the past.

She has shown me, how no matter what you have gone through you shouldn't victimize yourself. Instead you should raise your head high and look towards the future.

Because no matter what there is always a brighter future for you. She taught me how you can choose the path that you want to live. She went through some horrible situations during her childhood and adulthood.

But instead of letting that affect her and ruin her life. She fought against everything and ended up becoming a wonderful human being. She has accomplished so many things, and there is so many more things that she will accomplish. Because she has chosen to live a happier life. I hope to one day be able to accomplish all the things that she has accomplished. Not only in my personal life, but also in my Mary Kay career. Her name is Vernessa Blackwell. To me its Mommy she is an author in Tainted Elegance as well, I love and adore this Amazing Woman!

You are beautiful,
you are beautiful with make up on,
you are beautiful without it on,
and you are beautiful right after running miles on the treadmill.
You are beautiful when you are not smiling,
you are beautiful when you are smirking,
and you are beautiful when she is smiling.
You are beautiful inside,
you are beautiful out,
Your Beauty is magnificent
I love your uniqueness

You are so beautiful...

# About Takia Smith

Takia Smith is a member of Zion Wesley AME and the CEO of Dream Kiapers. Dream Kiapers is a non-profit organization helping young men and women with their dreams to prosper in the work force. If it means school, job or career with Kia's assistance anything is possible. Takia is also an Independent Beauty Consultant with Mary Kay.

As a young woman Takia, maintains the overwhelming life of a Soldier, Wife and devoted mom through her belief and trust in Jesus Christ. She has transformed into an awesome wife along with being a dedicated and encouraging mother of three beautiful children Khalil, Terrence and Kamille. Takia has a full time job as a DC Army National guard soldier and is a full-time college student at Strayer University. She is currenlty pursuing an Bachelor's Degree in Business Management. Takia would like to thank her husband Terrence, whose patience during this project was impeccable. Takia can be reached at dreamkiapers@gmail.com, or dreamkiapers@facebook.com, or tsmith95794@marykay.com. You can also visit my Mary Kay website @www.marykay.com/tsmith95794.

# BEAUTY
## By: Charlene Day

Beauty can be found in time.

*Valuing your time allows you to to go through the good and bad with grace. Valuing your time means positioning yourself, believing in yourself and investing in yourself. That can never happen if you don't appreciate time.*

*Often I have been put to the challenge of complaining or accepting the fact that I can't change time but I can change how I react to the time that has been given. My reaction is based on respect. I am reminded that there is a time and a season for everything. I stop to be apart of that season and dress accordingly.*

I want to challenge you to do the same and look beyond your current situation, and dress appropriately for your season by positioning, believing and investing in yourself. Some of the lessons I learned was ugly ones of who I was and who I was not. Nevertheless, they where lessons learned through time. When I say this, I say it loud because the company I'm currently partnered with has taught me all of these things, and some of those are repeated lessons in my life about positioning myself. What this means is taking advantage of opportunities when they come, just engrossing yourself within the opportunities as they come to you. Always believe in yourself, believe enough to know that you can do anything if you put your mind to it. You can grow your business; you can help others invest within your business, but you have to believe in yourself, believe more than anybody else will believe in you. You have to invest in yourself, just like you would in the stock markets; you choose a hot stock that has potential and watch it grow. You invest your time, invest into your family, but most importantly never forget to invest in yourself. You can do all this by reading books that change your mindset, taking a day to spend time alone listening and planning your next move, going to workshops that line up with your goals and surrounding yourself around people that are like minded.

The end result is that Spring always comes at the same time every year and it brings a beauty with it that blooms as a fruition of you preparing and appreciating time.

# About Charlene Day

Charlene E. Day, is The International Educational Advocate. She is a stay at home mompreneur, homeschooling parent, author, giver, speaker, who enjoys developing educational plans for parents, nonprofits and for profit organizations. She is known for her witty skills in collaborating efforts and speaking to audiences to overcoming fear.

# You God Driven Destiny
## By Cee Cee H. Caldwell-Miller, MA, CLC, ALS

I am sure you have heard the statement "Life is a series of choices." To some, that is too simple, but it really is true. Your decisions determine your destiny. Likewise, you make decisions every day that move you closer to your God-driven destiny—or away from it. There is no such thing as just sitting still or putting God's plan for your life on hold. That is a deception. God's will for your life is intertwined with His will for others, and that is a constantly moving and evolving dynamic. Every one of us has a God-driven destiny designed to touch others in a major way. We are carrying other people's miracles, connected to other people's dreams, visions and goals. We do not even realize it. I do not think we can fully comprehend this. It is certain, however, that the lives of people will be changed simply because we made the right decisions. Let me ask you a question, Are you certain that the decisions you are making every day are the ones the Lord wants you to make? If you cannot answer that with a yes, then what is preventing you from doing so? Most of you do not intentionally decide to miss your destinies. They just get busy, loaded down with the cares of this life, and before you know it, you are in a hole that you cannot seem to get out of on your own. You may have experienced major tragedies, trials and tribulations that may have stunted your progress toward the manifestation of your destiny. Nevertheless, remember, your life is the result of choices—YOUR choices. Others can influence or hinder you, but your choices are the determining factor of your destiny and they are also, what propels you into your future. It is never too late to make the right choices. Nevertheless, you must first take 100% responsibility for your life and be sure not to blame, make excuses for or just be a spectator in your life; you must CHOOSE to be a fully engaged active participant as you live the authentic life you were destined to live.

Your destiny is not a matter of chance; it is a matter of definite choice. It is not something you wait for, but rather something you pursue with everything that is within you. You are not to wait for extraordinary opportunities, you are to seize common occasions and make them great experiences everyday of your lives. Opportunities sometimes come masked in the form of misfortune or temporary defeat, trials, tribulations or struggles. The presence of setbacks is not what makes the difference in your life, but your response to handling them that matters the most and will create your future. Your setbacks are just setups for your comebacks. God expects you to handle the difficulties in your lives by using the Word of God as your Blueprint for living in this world as loving, compassionate, honorable and trustworthy human beings.

It is important to start where you are and move on from there. At this moment, you are standing right in the middle of an opportunity. It is up to you to decide how you will choose to you it. If you have goals, dreams and aspirations, you must now act on them. It is critical to understand that you are never given a dream from God without also being given the power to make it manifest. The achievement of your goal is assured the moment you commit yourself to God first and then to your dreams. If you have the burning desire, you have the power to attain it. You can have anything you want in life if you will sacrifice for it and if you will trust God to order your steps and lead you into your God Driven Destiny. Where there is God and a burning desire joined with faith, your future is limitless.

It is important to know that you are special, you been assigned to serve and you already possess the greatness within you to be a catalyst for change and to make a grand impact in this world. You must stand tall knowing that you can accomplish magnificent things that will impress upon others in your life to be and do their absolute best to make a difference in the lives of those around them.

To all of you who have suffered in any way in this life and are engaged in the rebuilding of your lives. I recommend that you DREAM bigger, FOLLOW your passion with purpose, Be true to and honor yourself, PERSEVERE no matter what, Be a solution creator, ENJOY your life to the fullest without regrets and let LOVE be your intent in all things. I know it is not easy to rebuild; this season might be difficult but if you are open & willing to grow, learn and love. You will find that your best days are indeed ahead of you, so quit looking in the rearview mirror of your past and ahead to your future. Live your best life in this very moment, being all that you can, putting forth every effort to accomplish everything that is within you and promising to LIVE FULL and DIE EMPTY! Press on to your God-driven destinies, NO MATTER WHAT it takes. Someone is waiting for the REAL YOU to show up in their lives and aid them in living their God Driven Destiny "You shall Encourage, Empower and Inspire humanity as you continue to walk by faith in your God Driven Destiny!"

# Undeniably Miserable
## By: Ashley Love

Lost! Searching for something I have NO CLUE.
Effortless, I lay BROKEN, BATTERED and BRUISED.
Torn apart in PIECES,
The reflection of me, I BARELY EVEN KNEW.
Once whole, now SHATTERED.
Bound by the notion, my life DIDN'T MATTER.
Helpless, Weak, Strength-lacking
Little HOPE, No FAITH, Negatively UNREACTIVE
Bitter and held painfully CAPTIVE
By the conversations in my mind
From those who spoke LIES
Worthless, Nothing and Never-Will-Be
A Loser, A Whore, A Nobody
Tears like a tune
Drip-Drop into a puddle.
Confidence non-existent,
Repercussions not SUBTLE.
Survival not EMINENT,
Seconds not FAVORABLE.
Down and out SILENCE,
Words not ABLE.
UNDENIABLY MISERABLE.

See, for years, I was miserable. I hated the reflection that I saw every time my eyes glanced into a mirror. I was chubby or maybe just plain fat. I was too white and when I tried to tan, I ended up burning up my body. My stomach was too flabby. My thighs were too big. My feet looked like skis.. Well, okay that's what they told me growing up. My hair was too straight, but not straight enough. I hated my nose and my face was pudgy.

See…I spent years hiding from myself telling myself that I wasn't good enough. I listened to people tell me all of my flaws and I focused only on them. I was MISERABLE, UNDENIABLY MISERABLE.

My confidence was non-existent and I was tearing myself down mentally. My lack of love for myself led me into bad relationships and negative choices. I believed I wasn't good enough. I lived in a bubble because I was so scared to be myself. I thought people would hate me or judge me.. maybe even make fun of me.

BUT ONE DAY…ONE DAY, I DECIDED TO MAKE A CHANGE… FOR ME…..

I was just beginning my career and was forced into the spotlight. Although, I am a writer and enjoy being behind the scenes, I realized that I had to step into the greatness that God had for me. I had to learn to love myself…to be confident in who I am and to stop allowing myself to hide from the world. If I was going to fulfill my dreams, I had to get over my negative self-chatter. I was talking myself out of success and out of opportunities. No one was holding me captive, but ME.

I started reciting affirmations daily in the mirror.

I AM…BEAUTIFUL
I AM …STRONG
I AM…WORTH BEING TREATED RIGHT
I AM…LOVE
I AM…RESPONSIBLE FOR MY OWN HAPPINESS
I AM…TAKING ACTION EVERYDAY TO GET TO KNOW MYSELF
I AM…WELCOMING AN ABUNDANCE OF POSITIVITY IN MY LIFE

I AM…STEPPING INTO MY GREATNESS
I AM…STRONGER THAN I BELIEVE
I AM…PERFECTLY TAINTED
I AM…ME AND THAT IS A BLESSING
I AM…THANKFUL TO GOD FOR CREATING ME IN THE IMAGE HE ENVISIONED ME TO BE
I AM…NOT BROKEN
I AM…A GORGEOUS WOMAN

See when you say "I AM", you are making a declaration of who you are and I had to change all of the negative I AM statements that were clouding my self-image into positives.

It did not change overnight and even on this very day, I still have my weak moments, but I choose to love who I am and in that very statement it gives me power to make decisions that only positively affect my life.

When you know who you are, you stand strongly in your own shoes. You then aren't willing to sacrifice your morals and your beliefs because you realize they make you who you are. The moment you decide to be confident in who you are, you decide to really start living.

As someone recently told me, "Ashley, I give you permission to be selfish sometimes." That statement was not meant in a negative way, but to say that I am free to think about me and my wants and needs sometimes and not just about others all the time.

As women, we are programmed to be caretakers and focus on others, but we must realize that we need time for ourselves as well. We cannot fulfil even the role of caretaker, if we are not taken care of ourselves. Give yourself time and something for you. Take a nice warm bath. Read a good book. Learn something you have been wanting to. Exercise or do yoga. Write your first (or next) book. Make time for what makes you happy and never stop believing that you can fulfill your dreams.

DECLARATION TO SELF:

I, _____, commit to loving who I am from this very moment forward. No matter what anyone else says about me, I will know and believe only the truth. I am a blessing from God to the world and I am made in the very image that God had for me. I am perfectly imperfect. Although I am tainted and scarred from the battles I have faced in life, I am simply beautiful. I will per sue my dreams with confidence in myself and my abilities. I will change my negative self-chatter to positive self-encouragement and I will never stop believing in myself and thanking God that I AM ME.

_____        _____/_____/_____
       Signature                            Date

# About The Compiler

**Ashley Love**

Ashley Love, known as the Visionary Mompreneur, is a best-selling author, publisher, business coach and activist…BUT her favorite role is mother to her three daughters. Previously published books include Tainted Elegance: In the Key of Love and Fearless Poets Against Bullying. Ashley also co-authored Head Ladies in Charge and I Am: Love, Wisdom & Guidance through Soul Reflection.

Ashley received the Distinguished Woman in her 20s Award by the YMCA and Young Female Entrepreneur of the Year Award by the Unstoppable Women in 2014.

Ashley's main goal is to give people an outlet to share their messages and to speak up for those people whose voices often go unheard.

**Connect With the Co-Authors**

Visit www.TaintedElegance.com to find out more
about the POSITIVE-ly Beautiful Co-Authors
in this book and to connect with them.

Use the hashtags, #TaintedElegance and #SimplyBeautiful
to share your story, message, and takeaways from the
book on Facebook, Twitter, and Instagram.

Visit our YOUTUBE Channel at www.youtube.com/taintedelegance
to see videos from the ladies in the book and
for your weekly inspiration.

# BE A CO-AUTHOR
# OF THE NEXT TAINTED ELEGANCE BOOK
# OR ANOTHER BLOOMING PEN
# PRESS & PROMOTIONS
# PRODUCTION!

Are you ready to share your message with the world?

Are you ready to use your self-expression to give others hope?

Do you have a story or poem that you know will touch lives?

Your story or message could be the key that
UNLOCKS someone else's PRISON!

Visit www.chargedvisions.com
to view upcoming Co-Author Opportunities!

www.ingramcontent.com/pod-product-compliance
Lightning Source LLC
Chambersburg PA
CBHW071723090426
42738CB00009B/1862